THE FRANCISCAN VIEW
OF THE HUMAN PERSON

SOME CENTRAL ELEMENTS

DAWN M. NOTHWEHR, O.S.F.

VOLUME THREE
THE FRANCISCAN HERITAGE SERIES

CFIT/ESC-OFM
2005

**This pamphlet is the third in
The Franciscan Heritage Series
sponsored by the
Commission on the Franciscan Intellectual Tradition
of the English-speaking Conference of the
Order of Friars Minor
(CFIT/ESC-OFM)**

General Editor
Joseph P. Chinnici, O.F.M.

Assistant Editor
Elise Saggau, O.S.F.

ISBN:
1-57659-202-2

Library of Congress Control Number:
2004117121

Printed and bound in the United States of America
BookMasters, Inc.
Mansfield, Ohio

TABLE OF CONTENTS

ABBREVIATIONS

The following abbreviations are used in the text to designate writings of Francis and early biographical sources for the life of Francis. Unless otherwise indicated, all references are from *Francis of Assisi: Early Documents*, three volumes, ed. Regis J. Armstrong, J. A. Wayne Hellmann, William J. Short (New York: New City Press, 1999, 2000, 2001). The abbreviations designating the writings of Clare and early biographical sources for the life of Clare are taken from *Clare of Assisi Early Documents*, ed. and trans. Regis J. Armstrong (St. Bonaventure, NY: Franciscan Institute Publications, 1993).

Writings of Francis:

Adm   The Admonitions
CtC   The Canticle of the Creatures
ER   The Earlier Rule
1LtF   The First Letter to the Faithful (The Earlier Exhortation
        to the Brothers and Sisters of Penance)
2LtF   The Second Letter to the Faithful (The Later Admoni-
        tion and Exhortation to the Brothers and Sisters of
        Penance)
LtOrd   A Letter to the Entire Order
SalV   A Salutation of Virtues
Test   The Testament

Early Biographical Sources:

1C   The Life of Saint Francis by Thomas of Celano
AC   The Assisi Compilation
LMj   The Major Legend by Bonaventure

Writings of Clare:

1LAg   The First Letter to Blessed Agnes of Prague (1234)
2LAg   The Second Letter to Blessed Agnes of Prague (1235)
3LAg   The Third Letter to Blessed Agnes of Prague (1238)
4LAg   The Fourth Letter to Blessed Agnes of Prague (1253)
RCl   The Rule (1253)
TestCl The Testament (1247-1253)

Early Sources Concerning Clare:

Proc   The Acts of the Process of Canonization (1253)
LegCl   The Legend of Saint Clare (1254-1255)
1PrPov The Privilege of Poverty of Pope Innocent III (1216)

GENERAL EDITOR'S INTRODUCTION

On behalf of the Commission for the Retrieval of the Franciscan Intellectual Tradition (CFIT), I present to you with great pleasure this third volume of The Franciscan Heritage Series–*The Franciscan View of the Human Person: Some Central Elements* by Dawn M. Nothwehr, O.S.F. The purpose of this volume, building on the reflections on the foundational themes of the first two volumes, is to elucidate in greater detail the theology of the human person as a starting point for contemporary belief and practice. The centrality in our faith tradition of the relationship between the Creator and all of creation and the reflection of the Trinity's glory in everything that is, so fundamental to the spiritual vision of Francis and Clare, is now undergoing a renaissance in our twenty-first century world. The present volume provides a fine stimulus for further reflection in this most important area, which addresses the issues of human dignity, divine and human mediation, freedom, mutuality and ethics.

Dr. Dawn M. Nothwehr, O.S.F., a sister of St. Francis of Rochester, Minnesota, is presently teaching at the Catholic Theological Union, Chicago, as Assistant Professor of Ethics and Director of the Master of Divinity Program. Having written extensively on the ethical category of mutuality in John Duns Scotus and edited a volume on Franciscans and the environment, she is eminently qualified to render a well founded but contemporary account of major themes in the Franciscan understanding of the person. It is our hope that readers will take this short work and, with careful and thoughtful study, perhaps under the guidance of a mentor, begin to plumb the spiritual depths of our inheritance and comprehend the important uniqueness of its intellectual expression. Through reflection, prayer, conversation and action, may we also explore these theological themes and find ways to express them in preaching, pastoral practice, the works of evangelization and community formation with friars, sisters and laity. Each chapter of the present volume contains some summary statements, and the whole concludes with questions which will aid in this process.

The Franciscan View of the Human Person takes its place within the context of a much larger Franciscan Heritage Series. Two volumes have already been published: Kenan B. Osborne, O.F.M., *The Franciscan Intellectual Tradition: Tracing Its Origins and Identifying Its Central Components* (2003) and Ilia Delio, O.S.F., *A Franciscan View of Creation: Learning to Live in a Sacramental World* (2003). Several volumes to be published in the near future will address the magisterial approbation of this intellectual heritage as a constitutive stream in the Roman Catholic Tradition, the Johannine and cosmic scriptural vision of Francis of Assisi and the Franciscan understanding of Trinity, Christ and sacraments. Subsequent volumes will move beyond strictly theological issues to consider the role of the laity in the articulation of the tradition, the historical evolution of the intellectual movement, the relationship between the movement's practice of poverty and its contribution to a new economy, and notions of reform and humanism.

While standing on its own, each volume is intended to identify basic themes and elaborate on those elements in the Franciscan intellectual synthesis that, in the judgment of the authors, can make a significant contribution to contemporary issues. No attempts are made to conflate the distinctive experiences of Francis and Clare, Bonaventure, the lay practitioners, Duns Scotus and others, but rather to present the major insights of each as they might appeal to a contemporary reader in the language of the twenty-first century.

A deeper and more self-consciously academic penetration of the themes may be found in the series of volumes sponsored by CFIT and containing the papers delivered at the annual Franciscan symposium at the Washington Theological Union. The contours of the whole project and the role of CFIT in the retrieval of the tradition may be further discovered at CFIT-ESC-OFM.org.

The Third Volume

In this larger context, I would like to call attention to the important interface between Dr. Nothwehr's volume, so well founded in the tradition's voice, and one pressing contemporary concern: **the exercise of freedom**.

In his encyclical letter of 1993, Pope John Paul II calls attention to the importance of *freedom as a constituent element of human dignity*:

> Human freedom belongs to us as creatures; it is a freedom which is given as a gift, one to be received like a seed and to be cultivated responsibly. It is an essential part of that creaturely image which is the basis of the dignity of the person. Within that freedom there is an echo of the primordial vocation whereby the Creator calls man [men and women] to the true Good, and even more, through Christ's Revelation, to become his friend and to share his own divine life. It is at once inalienable self-possession and openness to all that exists, in passing beyond self to knowledge and love of the other. Freedom then is rooted in the truth about man [men and women], and it is ultimately directed towards communion (86).

This focus on freedom as an essential part of human dignity, its reality as a gift from God, its embededness in the creaturely and often sinful human condition, and the sign of its true fruition in communion with God, others and the world has significant implications for the times in which we live. How do we value our freedom? How do we apply it in politics, economics and ethics? How do we freely govern, both in the society and in the Church, so as to value the multiplicities of peoples and freedoms that God has created in the world and also the diversities of peoples and freedoms that God has given to the Church? In a sinful world, what disciplines are needed so that freedom grows towards love of God, neighbor and self? These are the great challenges before us today.

In the Franciscan understanding of the person, this fundamental reality of human freedom is related to the will and its innate ability to choose or not to choose to engage the world, the neighbor, the task at hand, the creaturely condition in a way that is loving, affirming and constructive, giving glory to God in the image of whose freedom and communion we are made. While *The Franciscan View of the Human Person* directly reflects on the philosophy and theology of freedom and its relationship to knowledge in John Duns Scotus (see Part Four), the true human path of freedom is indicated throughout:

- In reflections on Francis and Clare and how they used freedom without coercion in serving the poor and recognizing their dignity and in practicing mutual charity in community;
- In reflections on the Eucharist as a sign of how Christ as both God and man chooses to use his freedom to nourish others through humility and mercy and to place his own work and energy at the service of his neighbor's life;
- In our human experience of daily limitation and death and how the arena of our earthly life's diminishment can become, by following in the footprints of Christ, not a place of fear but a doorway to risen life and communion with others;
- In Bonaventure's view of the unsurpassed dignity of the human person, under grace, as one called to participate in God's own life and mystery.

Human dignity and freedom are spoken about here in multiple languages: the literary language of biography, metaphor and story; the philosophical language of ontology and metaphysics; the performative language of ethics and service; the religious language of conversion. Again, at these fundamental levels there is a consistent link between the vernacular language of Francis and Clare and the school languages of Bonaventure and Scotus. Religious experience, philosophical analysis, theological reflection, communal witness and social project are of one piece.

Dr. Nothwehr's volume has multiple applications. She deftly founds our embodied human condition, the ethical demand of mediation, the fundamental dimension of relationality and humankind's social project of loving kinship in the Franciscan Trinitarian and Christological vision. She touches in a systematic way the basic argument in which the contemporary world is engaged: *What does it mean to be human? What does it mean to be free?*

Again, we find convergence here with the words of John Paul II:

> *Our faith is profoundly anthropological,* rooted constitutively in coexistence, in the community of God's people, and in *communion with this eternal "THOU."* Such coexistence is essential to our Judeo-Christian tradition and comes from God's initiative. This initiative is connected with and leads to creation, and is at the same time—as Saint Paul teaches—"the eter-

nal election of [men and women] in the Word who is the Son." (*Crossing the Threshold of Hope*, 1994, p. 36).

It is CFIT's conviction that the performed path of Francis and Clare following in the footprints of Christ and the formulated path expressed by Bonaventure and Scotus hold out for today some treasured insights into these most basic truths.

Making Connections

The Commission for the Retrieval of the Franciscan Intellectual Tradition hopes that some teachers and practitioners will translate the basic themes presented in this volume into still more popular forms and make them accessible to an ever-wider public of interested parties. CFIT would like to sponsor two-page summaries and updates, in printed and web-page format, which might help form preaching, meditation and community conversation and serve as an even more practical illustration of basic principles. Each person and each "community of learning" has a different role to play in the larger project. May the Lord, in an ever-deeper fashion, show each of us a way to make these profound insights and truths life-giving in our Church and society.

Joseph P. Chinnici, O.F.M.
Franciscan School of Theology
Berkeley, California 94709
Ordinary Time, 2005

PART ONE
AUTHOR'S INTRODUCTION

The internationally renowned ethicist, Daniel C. Maguire, centers his understanding of Christian moral life on the maxim: "The foundational moral experience is reverence for human persons and their environment."[1] This fundamental insight that underlies Maguire's ethics sings in harmony with what the Franciscan tradition claims about the human person, and it is through the lens of this insight that I read the Franciscan tradition. More importantly, however, the Franciscan tradition illuminates Maguire's basic insight.

There is a sense of the sacredness of human life, though expressed in numerous ways, which lies at the heart of every human culture around the globe. We assign value to persons as persons. This sacredness is not something that can be proven in a laboratory or through a logical syllogism. The inviolable dignity of the human person is known through the wisdom of the heart. Such wisdom is profoundly intuitive, affective and empathetic. Such is the wisdom of love meeting Love. This is the great truth of the Franciscan view of the human person: God, who is Love and the Source of All Goodness, created humans and called them "very good" (Gen. 1:31). Though humans sinned, that sin did not determine the relationship between God and humans. The God of Love chose to reveal divine love in the Incarnation–God become flesh in the person of Jesus. Subsequently, humanity is graced with the means of salvation made visible through the teachings of Jesus, the example of his love for his *Abba* and the experience of this transforming offer of love.

Some look to the negative side of human experience with revulsion, holding a cynical attitude toward human failures and limitations, stressing sin and death. But even this very revulsion signals the possibility for a deeper goodness. It is possible to learn of the Good by contrast with the evil. But why work so hard to learn what is so obvious? Beginning with St. Francis and St. Clare of Assisi, Franciscans choose to define the human person in relationship to the great Love who is God.

In Christ and through the Incarnation, God chose to deify human existence.[2] From the moment of their creation, humans

1

are without equal in the world (Gen. 1:26-27 and Gen. 2:7). They are personal subjects, capable of being self-reflexive; that is, they are able to realize and reflect on the reality that they are conscious beings. They are capable of comprehending that they can make choices to be or act in a certain way and why they choose to do so. This is the primary way that human persons are distinct from other creatures in creation–from plants, other animals, or inanimate things. Most distinctive is the reality that humans can have a "face to face" personal relationship with God, because God chose to communicate with them by coming to live on Earth as a human being, Jesus of Nazareth. Humanity was honored in this way; but most importantly, this condescension of God also made it possible for fallen sinful humans to be restored, forgiven and made whole and holy through Christ. In this sense, because of the Incarnation–God taking on humanness and living among us–humanity was deified (made God-like).

It is humankind that now faces the dilemma concerning whether to choose life or to choose death (Deut. 30:15-18). The Franciscan way is to choose life and love. It is to let go of the egotistic pride of individualism and the fear of failure and to open the human heart to God's longing and loving embrace. Then, as one loved beyond measure, the beloved of God turns outward to the world–to family, friends, associates, the quarrelsome ones, the despicable and the despised, and, yes, even in an age of terrorism, to the enemy–and seeks to love them into life. This is the challenge, the possibility and the great hope that the Franciscan understanding of the human person holds out to the world.

This brief volume will discuss several of the central elements or most significant characteristics of human persons as found in those works of the Franciscan theological tradition which, when taken together, most sufficiently describe these qualities. As the tradition developed over the years, the intuitions and insights of St. Francis and St. Clare of Assisi concerning the human person were developed and/or restated in language better understood by the people of a particular era. Indeed, two of the most famous early Franciscan theologians, St. Bonaventure and Bl. John Duns Scotus, did just that. It is our intention, also, that this volume will, by drawing on the wisdom of the Franciscan tradition, contribute in a similar way to an understanding of the human person today.

The first chapter will discuss the central elements of the Franciscan understanding of human person, beginning with the founding intuitions of St. Francis and St. Clare. For these saints of Assisi, four major characteristics can be discerned:

1. Because humans are creatures created in God's image and likeness, *each person bears an inviolable dignity.*
2. Authentic humanness requires that this *dignity be made concrete and embodied* in daily human life. Just as God made known divine love "in the flesh" through the person of Jesus, so, too, must we humans bring our belief in human dignity to bear on the ordinary activities of daily life.
3. *Humans are creatures of the earth who live in relationship* with all of creation.
4. As finite creatures, *humans ultimately need to embrace bodily death* as part of life.

The second chapter will focus on the contributions of St. Bonaventure of Bagnoregio to the Franciscan understanding of the human person. Building on the fundamental intuitions of St. Francis and St. Clare concerning human dignity and embodiment, Bonaventure used the insights and vocabulary of the University of Paris in the thirteenth century to present the *human person as the similitude of God* in the created world. Humans have their origin in the love of the Triune God who gifts them with the capacities and the obligation to live in a unique relationship with God (soul), on the one hand, and with all of creation (body), on the other. Because of their unique capacities, *humans stand as mediators between God and the created world* and must live in relationship to both God and all of creation, such that all flourish. Though humans abused their freedom and sinned, God, through the passion of Christ incarnate, graced them with the possibility of returning to relationship with the divine. It is the on-going challenge of humans to live into the fullness of this grace by becoming more like Christ.

The contribution of Bl. John Duns Scotus to the Franciscan understanding of the human person is the focus of chapter three. Scotus, writing in the fourteenth century, used the scholastic discipline of philosophy to articulate his understanding of the human person.

However, he was a true son of Francis and Clare and thus demonstrates in his work some of the basic themes of human dignity, embodiment, relationship and mediation. However, Scotus brings greater specificity to the source of human dignity, to the kind of relationship we need to have with both God and creatures and to the way in which we are able to participate in God's grace to overcome sin. At Scotus's hand, we see that to be human is to be *uniquely* God's and called to live in *mutual* relationship with God, with other humans, with all creatures and with the entire cosmos.

All the chapters will draw out some contemporary applications of the particular characteristics of the human person as they are uncovered by each of the above Franciscans. It is my hope that in some small way this exposé of the Franciscan view of the human person might serve to reawaken the "miracle of real presence" that lies in each of us and in our human sisters and brothers.[3] We are all bearers of the image of God (*imago Dei*)–life deified through the Incarnation, God manifest in human flesh.

PART TWO
HUMANS–CREATURES BELOVED
OF GOD IN CHRIST

SOME CENTRAL ELEMENTS IN
ST. FRANCIS AND ST. CLARE OF ASSISI

INTRODUCTION

Francis and Clare of Assisi were friends who experienced a change of heart (conversion) and left lives promising prestige and wealth in order to "follow in the footprints of Jesus." There are many similarities in the way they each understood the human person and the relationship between God, humans and all of creation.

Both Francis and Clare were affected by the influences of the historical period in which they lived. Following the Gregorian Reform and the directives of the Synod of Rome (1059), during the eleventh and twelfth centuries, there were numerous religious and social movements throughout Europe that stressed a return by ordinary people to a renewed way of living the Gospel. These movements called people to the Scriptures, to a rejection of material wealth and even, in some cases, to life in community.[4] Among these groups were the Cathari, heretical Christians who espoused the dualistic belief that all material things are evil and all things of the spirit, good. The Cathari reasoned (contrary to the Catholic doctrine of the Incarnation) that Jesus, who is divine (spirit), could not *also* be really human (matter). Indeed, all things of the flesh or of matter are evil, including, for example, the human body, marriage and conception. The Assisi area was a hotbed of Catharism, and, in 1203, a member of the movement was even elected the town's mayor.

Certainly Francis and Clare, in their young adult years,[5] would have been aware of the Cathari and their beliefs disparaging the human body. In addition, Francis most certainly was aware of the

5

fact that the Church, at the Fourth Lateran Council (1215),[6] condemned the dualism of the Cathari as "heretical." It is widely held by Franciscan scholars that, because of these influences and because there were some similarities between the way of life of the Cathari and of the early Franciscans, both Francis and Clare stressed certain aspects of Christian doctrine and were careful to seek the approval of their Rules from the Church. There is in fact some evidence that John of St. Paul, the Church official who presented Francis to the Roman Curia and assisted him in getting his first Rule approved, was well aware of the Church's need for the Franciscans to teach and witness to a faithful understanding of Jesus and the human person.[7] Francis and Clare, so as not to be confused with the Cathari and other heretical groups, stressed the following doctrinal notions: God gave humans their *whole* body and their *whole* soul; Jesus was born from the womb of Mary, a human mother; Jesus shed real drops of human blood during his passion.[8]

Francis and Clare were also influenced by the general understanding of a common spiritual practice of the time known as "asceticism." In an effort to come closer to God and to become better Christians, people would fast, choose to do unnecessary rigorous physical work, or even harm their flesh. This practice was understood not so much as a rejection of the physical human body, but rather as a means of bringing the whole person to greater Christian perfection.[9] The general idea was that Christians should not be self-indulgent, but rather give attention to spiritual matters and Christian living.

We can see that, from time to time, Francis and Clare seemed to embrace extremes and to contradict what they taught concerning asceticism.[10] Such inconsistency, rather than casting doubt on the witness of these saints, can, in fact, make it more believable. The balance of evidence shows their intent was to be faithful to the doctrines of Creation, Redemption and Incarnation as the basis for calling the human body good.

While Francis and Clare were influenced by the culture and religious practices of their time and place, they were most faithful to the *full* Gospel and the teaching of the Church concerning the human person. They both upheld significant aspects or characteristics of what is authentically human. The four major characteristics we will examine here are:

1. Humans are created in the image and likeness of God and thus each bears an inviolable dignity.
2. Authentic humanness requires that this dignity be made concrete and embodied in daily living.
3. Though they have a distinct inviolable dignity, humans are earth creatures who live among other creatures of the earth.
4. Bodily death is part of human life.

We will first address these four aspects from the viewpoint of Francis and then make a similar examination of the four aspects from the viewpoint of Clare.

FRANCIS OF ASSISI AND THE HUMAN PERSON

What enabled Francis to break from the negative influences of his culture was his personal experience of Jesus. From Francis's own writings and from the biographies written by Thomas of Celano and by St. Bonaventure, we can glean two important themes that flowed from this experience and shaped Francis's understanding of what it means to be a human person. First, Francis was thoroughly enamored of the profound humility of God, demonstrated in the Incarnation–God taking on humanness and living among us (1C 84).[11] Secondly, for Francis, the passion of Christ illustrated in the most powerful way God's unfathomable, abiding and unconditional love for humans, indeed for the entire world. Like a parent who, out of deep love does not give up on an errant child, God does not give up on humanity when people sin. God does not break the divine-human bond. Instead, Jesus, the Son of God, freely chooses to suffer and die on the cross.

The Incarnation and Human Dignity

The humility of the Incarnation pointed Francis toward a distinct manner of understanding the human person. Because God became human in Jesus Christ, all of humanity was deified (*deificet*), i.e., graced by God and given access to become God-like.[12] Francis saw

Jesus as the model human being, who set the standard and marked the way for all other humans to travel on the journey of daily life toward the fullness of life with God. The human imagination could grasp the possibility of a life with God by observing Jesus' union with his *Abba*–God the Father. Clearly, Jesus was like us, and we humans could see that there was also something about us that could be like Jesus. What a gift this realization is for a fallen humanity! How profoundly this gift restored human dignity! In unfathomable wisdom, God chose to use the means of our very humanity to communicate great divine love for us. As Francis explained: "Though He was rich, He wished, together with the most Blessed Virgin, His mother, to choose poverty in the world beyond all else" (2LtF 5). What human being is not moved by the beauty and innocence of a baby? As an artist knows his or her work most intimately, so too, God knows how best to communicate boundless love to humanity.

Thus, in the stable at Bethlehem, humanly concrete things began to communicate the profound love of God for us. It was the physical, embodied discomfort of an infant in a manger that profoundly moved Francis and provided him with the best understanding of the marvelous overflowing love of God. It enabled him to recognize the capacity of humanity, deified and dignified by the humility of God in the Incarnation, to continue to tell that story of Love in this world. It was Francis's experience of his own dignity flowing from this exquisite and fecund love of God, shown in the Incarnation, that would later lead him to proclaim:

> Let us all love the Lord God Who has given and gives to each one of us our whole body, our whole soul and our whole life, Who has created, redeemed and will save us by His mercy alone, Who did and does everything good for us, miserable and wretched, rotten and foul, ungrateful and evil ones. Therefore, let us desire nothing else, let us want nothing else, let nothing else please us and cause us delight except our Creator, Redeemer and Savior, the only true God, Who is the fullness of good, all good, every good, the true and supreme good, *Who alone is good*, merciful, gentle, delightful, and sweet, Who alone is holy, just, true, holy and upright, Who alone is kind, innocent, clean, from Whom, *through Whom* and in Whom is all pardon, all grace, all glory

of all the penitents and just ones, of all the blessed rejoicing together in heaven (ER 8b-9).

So Francis organized the first living Nativity scene in the town of Greccio to help people see, in real life and in their own time and place, what the love of God looks like and the extent to which God would go to restore human dignity (1C 84-6). In the scene at Greccio, we see the generous love of God made concrete, but also the marvelous capacity of humanity–even an unsophisticated baby–to communicate that love. Like a parent, who out of love freely chooses to suffer with or for a child so that the child might grow and be empowered to come to full maturity, so too God chose to love humanity into life.

Thus, Francis understood humanity as good and uniquely beloved of God, bearing the divine image and likeness and an inviolable dignity from the moment of creation. This image of God is found in *all* humans. It is reverence for the life of God, present in each person, and the fact that Jesus came to us in human form that stirred in Francis a profound reverence for all human life. He wrote, admonishing his followers:

> Consider, O human being, in what excellence the Lord God has placed you, for He created and formed you to the image of His Beloved Son according to the body and to His own likeness according to the Spirit (Adm 5:1).

The Passion and Human Dignity

Yet, the loving God created humans with freedom, and there was always the possibility that they would break the love connection with God. That, indeed, happened; humans sinned (Gen. 3). Though they are endowed with an inviolable dignity, humans are mixed in their capacity for good or for ill. Francis recognized this as he continued in his admonition:

> And all the creatures under heaven serve, know, and obey their Creator, each according to its own nature, better than you. And even the demons did not crucify Him, but you together with them, having crucified Him are still crucifying Him by delighting in vices and sins (Adm 5:2-3).

In Francis's view, the fall into sin was linked to human self-will. Therefore, humans deserve to be punished (Adm 2:3-5). However, God did not punish humans as they deserved, but instead, initiated a divine plan of salvation. As the biblical record of salvation history shows, time and time again when humanity sins, God is there to forgive the repentant sinner and to offer another chance. The most powerful statement of this love is the image of the crucified Christ. Francis expressed his deep joy and gratitude for the gift of God's love in these words: "O how holy and how loving, gratifying, humbling, peace-giving, sweet, worthy of love, and above all things, desirable: to have such a Brother and such a Son, our Lord Jesus Christ, Who laid down His life for His sheep" (1LtF 1:13). For Francis it was the virtue of obedience, of listening to God's voice speaking to us through the Scriptures, through one another and through all of the elements and creatures of creation, that enables us to return and to stay rooted in life with God (SalV 14).

Eucharist and Human Dignity

God's passionate love for and affirmation of the dignity of fallen humanity is also consistently offered to us in a marvelous and intimate way in the Eucharist. The Eucharist can be understood as a continuation of the Incarnation and the ongoing fruit of the passion. In each Eucharist, Catholics believe, the Christ becomes present to us. By participating in the Eucharist, we are united with Christ and share deeply in God's love and saving power. The bread, the wine and the human–each in its own way is made holy and whole through the presence of Christ. Each communicant is affirmed and given the grace to live into her or his God-given dignity. In Francis's understanding, to fail to show proper reverence for Christ present in the Eucharist or Christ present in the human person is also to blaspheme the other. Francis expressed his utter wonder at this marvelous manifestation of God's love this way:

> O wonderful loftiness and stupendous dignity! O sublime humility! O humble sublimity! The Lord of the Universe, God and the Son of God, so humbles Himself that for our salvation He hides Himself under an ordinary piece of bread! (LtOrd 27).[13]

It was this kind of utter self-emptying love (*kenosis*) that Francis recognized at the core of Christ's influence over the human heart. Human dignity is established in the Incarnation, confirmed through the Passion and nurtured in the Eucharist.

Human Dignity Embodied:
Following in the Footprints of Jesus

For Francis, the Incarnation, the Passion, and the Eucharist were not just idle beliefs. To the contrary, they were real events that grounded the embodiment of human dignity in concrete actions and attitudes. Francis was thus drawn to "follow in the footprints of Jesus" and he learned the depths of human dignity through the mercy of God.

Jesus did not force or coerce anyone to follow him. Rather, Jesus simply and unreservedly loved, letting go of personal power so that others might find their own power. Perhaps the most notable aspect of the life and ministry of Jesus is that he spent no time seeking prestige, but he constantly interacted with ordinary people, especially the powerless poor, widows and children of his day. In freedom, humans can choose to respond to love or reject it. Paradoxically, as Francis learned by following Jesus, when humans surrender to love, they are most powerful and most free.

Human Dignity and the Mercy of God

Indeed, to be human is to be limited in many ways. Yet, God's mercy transformed and empowered the Poverello to live beyond those limits. The poor Christ drew Francis in from the very earliest days of his conversion. Disillusioned by the effects of war and the grab for power between Assisi and Perugia, Francis searched for what he should do with his life. It was when Francis met a leper and felt compelled to embrace him in all of his weakness and despicable smelly ugliness, that Francis was transformed. Francis later explained:

> The Lord gave me, Brother Francis, thus to begin doing penance in this way: for when I was in sin, it seemed too bitter for me to see lepers. And the Lord Himself led me among

them and *I showed mercy* to them. And when I left them, what had seemed bitter to me was turned to sweetness of soul and body (Test 1-2).

Clearly, God was instrumental in enabling Francis to embrace the very kind of human being he had only despised in his youth. Now, through the grace of God, Francis understood that it is not physical beauty, material wealth, military might, or political influence that makes people valuable. Rather, it is the dignity that each person bears as one created in the image of God and unconditionally loved and redeemed by God in Christ that properly determines human worth. We are obligated to reverence this dignity by actions and attitudes that embody respect for each human person.

Thereafter, following the poor and humble Christ, Francis spent much of his time with the likes of lepers, who were the outcasts of his society. In every way possible Francis lived as Jesus lived. Just as the crucified Christ, out of tremendous love for humanity, humbly served people, so too Francis "showed deeds of humility and humanity to the lepers with a gentle piety. He visited their houses frequently, generously distributed alms to them, and with a great drive of compassion kissed their hands and their mouths" (LMj 1:6). Following the example of Christ, who was fully human and who embraced our human flesh and our human weakness, Francis was willing and able to physically touch and embrace the untouchables of his day, because he believed that all humans deserve reverence. In all of this, Francis embodied human dignity.

Francis also showed us that humanity, at its best, continues to bear Christ to the world in the usual events of life. Today, in our vast depersonalized cyber societies, it is often through small "random act of kindness" or simply speaking up on behalf of someone less assertive that lives can be changed, because human dignity is made concrete. Perhaps, for most of us, it is in the routine and mundane things of life that God's presence is most needed. We can follow Francis's example, finding ordinary ways that God's image (*imago Dei*) and God's love can shine forth in us and for others.

Human Dignity and the Poor

Like Francis, all Christians need to seek justice for the poor, because the poor have a right to basic human dignity, life and sustenance.

Francis was clear that the poor do not have to prove they are "deserving." Rather, as Francis asserts:

> Alms are the legacy and a justice due to the poor that our Lord Jesus Christ acquired for us. The brothers who work at acquiring them will receive a great reward and enable those who give them to gain and acquire one; for all that people leave behind in the world will perish, but they will have a reward from the Lord for the charity and almsgiving they have done (ER 9:8-9).

In fact, contrary to some of the beliefs of his day (for example, that the poor were extraordinarily sinful and therefore their poverty was a punishment from God), Francis defended the poor as those who rightly claim our love in a special way, insofar as they are living reminders of the poor Christ. Therefore, according to Thomas of Celano:

> [Francis] used to say: "Anyone who curses the poor insults Christ whose noble banner the poor carry, since Christ *made himself poor for us in this world.*" That is also why, when he met poor people burdened with wood or other heavy loads, he would offer his weak shoulders to help them. The holy man overflowed with the spirit of charity, bearing within him a deep sense of concern not only toward other humans in need but also toward mute, brute animals: reptiles, birds, and all other creatures whether sensate or not (1C 76-77).

Embracing the Human Dignity of the "Other"

But there are many ways human dignity is quashed, and there are no two people alike. In the vast diversity of creation, there will always be some people who are easier for us to get along with than others. It is so easy to get caught up in the competitiveness of a situation or relationship and find ways to distinguish ourselves and diminish others. To some degree, competition can bring out the best in us. Yet, when we find ourselves losing the perspective of our common human dignity–the reality of the divine image and likeness borne by each and every person–then competition ceases to be worthy of our participation. How we treat those we perceive as different from ourselves can form the basis for creating lasting bonds of friendship or it can become the occasion for war. The ultimate "other" is our "enemy." Francis explicitly challenged his followers, both by what he said and by what he did, to see their common humanity with others and to use negative experiences as occasions for growth, rather than seek revenge. Francis challenged:

> All my brothers: let us pay attention to what the Lord says: *Love your enemies* and *do good to those who hate you,* for our Lord Jesus Christ, Whose footprints we must follow, called His betrayer friend and willingly offered Himself to His executioners. Our friends, therefore, are all those who unjustly inflict upon us distress and anguish, shame and injury, sorrow and punishment, martyrdom and death. We must love them greatly for we shall possess eternal life because of what they bring us (ER 22:1-4).

Francis's secret to being so open to others was the security he felt because of his relationship with Christ. Indeed, it is the governing factor in understanding his kinship to all creatures. His insight into the three-dimensional relationship–humans and God, God and creatures, humans and creatures–was unique. The common relationship of both humans and other creatures with God makes humans and all creatures sisters and brothers–and that makes all the difference!

Human Dignity and Human Creaturehood

At the time when he wrote the beginning part of the *Canticle of the Creatures,*[14] Francis was marked with the stigmata, a sign of the profound intimacy of his identification with Jesus.[15] He was near the end of his life, weak, and suffering from a painful eye disease that left him sensitive to light and almost blind. Thomas Murtaugh concludes: "It is from this position of pain and peace that the *Canticle* makes sense; pain, because it can purify, clear away the dross and the unessential, and make clear the basics; peace, because without peace of heart, how could anyone who was suffering at all compose such limpid, lyrical lines."[16]

Eric Doyle shows us the process and the dynamics of Francis's journey toward this realization of the kinship of all creation.[17] As

Doyle points out, Francis, the poet-mystic, used words in ways that point beyond the usual meanings assigned them. In the *Canticle* we not only have beautiful poetic praise of the God of all creation, but an "expression of the authentic Christian attitude toward creation which is to accept and love the creatures as they are."[18] All created beings are expressions of the goodness and love of God. In our own creaturehood, we humans are equal with all other creatures. In fact, in the Covenant, God purposefully established a relationship not only with humans, but also with *every living creature* (Gen. 9:12-13). Similar to humans, whose dignity comes from God, other creatures are unique reflections of God and God's goodness. As God loves each creature uniquely, so too must we. Francis could know this divine way because he first entered into a contemplative union with God; he knew God in and through all other beings and elements of creation. In union with God and all creatures, Francis found his uniqueness as one human person, ever more original–a being with an inviolable dignity.

Francis's realization of both his uniqueness among the creatures and his likeness to them as a recipient of the love of God was a source of his great love of God's creation. To reflect on this immersion in love is to encounter Mystery, "the 'never-the-last-wordness' of our existence."[19] Humans are always seeking and searching for "something more." Our every attempt to satisfy the "more" ends in more seeking. Francis's "heart sight" told him he had found the "more" in God; and God was ever present here and now and all around him.

The words of the *Canticle* express integration in Francis's inner depths. As Doyle holds: "All beautiful words and music come from the mystery of personhood, welling up from the inner depths. It is not so remarkable that Francis, though blind, was able to write a song about the beauty and unity of creation. He was already one with himself and with the world, and the world was one in him."[20] This integration provided Francis with inner confidence and a cure for alienation from any and all "others" that could pose a threat to him. The path to such integration for Francis was a path of prayer that began with the first step of self-surrender.

The biography of Francis tells the story of his struggle to embrace poverty as a way of opening himself in freedom to God and all creation. Through his relationship with God in prayer, he learned to love *as* and *what* God loves. To love authentically is to accept other humans and all creatures on their own terms. It is particularly significant for our ecologically threatened world that Francis was able to find himself and true peace and harmony, not in warfare or wealth, but through spiritual means. He contemplated Christ and was in conscious communion with God manifested in creation. In coping with the spiritual malaise of our own time, prayer and spiritual practices are necessary to assist us in reversing warfare, terrorism and the devastation of the planet.[21] This is not escapism, but rather a move to the depths of our being. We need to confront the deepest truth of being human, namely, that we are creatures who stand in relationship with God, with the human family and with all earth creatures. When we realize we are not alone, but surrounded with wondrous manifestations of God's love and care, personal integration can take place and alienation vanishes.

Embracing Sister Death as Part of Human Life

To understand humanity's relationship to all of creation through prayer and contemplation is also a political act. To be in a love relationship with people and all of creation is to risk being motivated to act in defense and protection of those we love. We cannot tolerate injustice or abuse of persons and their environment because all creatures are our sisters and our brothers. When we are motivated to defend another, our focus shifts from self to the other. It is often risky to be so motivated; it is a move toward poverty, indeed perhaps the ultimate poverty of losing our own life for the sake of another.

Quite significantly, and in a more personal way, Francis even called death, "Sister," for he understood death as integral to human life. Indeed, death is the ultimate journey into poverty, a letting go of all possessions including life itself (LMj 14:2). Having given his life completely to Christ, Francis had nothing to fear from death. Death was for him a human passage into the fullness of life with Christ. In our day fear of the "small deaths" of life, such as personal limitations or the inability to achieve wealth or position, is frequently the cause of discord, abuse, or other kinds of violence. We can learn much from Francis's embrace of death as a "Sister" who opens the way to new life beyond our imagination. Would that we all, like

Francis, could embrace Sister Death singing praises as we are being drawn home into the very heart of God, the One who made us and loved us into life (AC 99). [22]

CLARE OF ASSISI
AND THE HUMAN PERSON

Unfortunately, there are very few works written by Clare's hand,[23] but we do have several letters and some documents related to the founding of the Poor Ladies (also called Poor Clares or Order of St. Clare). Through these documents we can see how Clare understood human beings, how she saw herself in relationship with others and what she expected of people, especially her sisters. Like Francis, Clare regarded human life as sacred because of the Incarnation–the great love of God displayed in the Passion of Christ. She recognized the deep communion that the Eucharist celebrates between God and human persons and human persons with their neighbors and all of creation. Yet, Clare lived out these beliefs in her own unique way together with her sisters.

The greatest influence in the life of Clare of Assisi was her experience of the "poor Christ" of the Gospels. Even before she met Francis, Clare was known for her piety and devotion.[24] However, having heard Francis preaching and after meeting with him privately, she recognized her vocation to a contemplative life of prayer.[25] Her calling was to live out her deep unquenchable desire to grow spiritually and to follow the footprints of Jesus in the enclosure of the monastery at San Damiano[26]

Clare's cloistered life is often difficult for present day Christians to imagine or understand because, for most of us, *our* everyday lives are filled with activities, sights and sounds that constantly bombard us and keep us very busy. Yet, all of us have had the experience of "I want *something* so bad I can taste it!" It was that kind of intensity of wanting and longing that Clare experienced in her relationship with Christ. When we know such an insatiable desire, there is *nothing* else that will satisfy us other than to achieve or acquire *the object* of our desire. It was like this with Clare and the Poor Ladies. They intensely pursued an intimate relationship with Christ. In light of their profound and central desire, the more significant standards of success in the Christian life, such as preaching and teaching, shifted. For Clare and the Poor Ladies, success was measured by intangible or transparent realities–spiritual growth, kindness, transformation and conversion of heart.

Clare was a student of Francis, and her understanding of the human person was similarly shaped by the Gospel. The Incarnation, the Passion of Christ and the Eucharist were for Clare–as for Francis–particularly revelatory. Yet, it was Clare's unique vocation and contribution to the Franciscan way of life to stress the "interior" dimensions of these aspects of Christian faith in ways that affected her life, her worldview and the lives of countless other people over the centuries. As Regis J. Armstrong puts it: "She took the Gospel insights offered by her teacher and recast them in a new, demanding form, thereby showing us in her clear, transparent way the Spirit of the Gospel Love that animated her."[27]

Clare was particularly attracted to Jesus as the "poor Christ" of the Gospels, and she tried to imitate him and stay focused on him. Poverty was the central dimension of the Gospel in Clare's view. She was convinced that living in strict material poverty was the way she and the Poor Ladies could best conform their lives to Christ. But, while she believed that living in austere poverty helps a person focus on Christ, she understood that the Gospel demands above all a transformation of heart, something God alone can bring about.

Francis and the brothers traveled the world as poor itinerants, preaching and doing works of mercy, supporting themselves by working and begging. Clare, however, and the Poor Ladies who lived at San Damiano and elsewhere were totally dependent on the care and generosity of others. While the friars wisely planned for the future of their missions and ministries, Clare and the Poor Ladies courageously and patiently counted on the Lord, showing profound faith in God's love, care and providence. Here we have two distinct expressions of the Franciscan tradition; yet in Clare's form of life we can find grounding for the same four positive aspects of the human person as we found in Francis. We will now examine these aspects as expressed in Clare's life and teaching:

1. Humans are created in the image and likeness of God and thus each bears an inviolable dignity.

2. Authentic humanness requires that this dignity be made concrete and embodied in daily living.
3. Though they have a distinct inviolable dignity, humans are earth creatures who live among other creatures of the earth.
4. Bodily death is part of human life.

The Incarnation and Human Dignity

The image of Christ closest to Clare's heart was that of "the God who was placed poor in the crib, lived poor in the world, and remained naked on the cross" (TestCl 45).[28] In her Fourth Letter to Agnes of Prague, Clare expressed her utter amazement that the glorious Son of God would be laid in a lowly crib:

> Look at the border of this mirror, that is, the poverty of Him Who was placed in a manger, wrapped in swaddling clothes. O marvelous humility! O astonishing poverty! The king of angels, the Lord of heaven and earth, is laid in a manger! (4LAg 19-21).[29]

This is the story of the Incarnation. The generous love of God is expressed in human flesh. For humans to be so loved is to be honored and graced with dignity beyond measure. As Clare recommended to Agnes of Prague, the only proper response to this marvelous affirmation of our humanity is to ". . . let yourself be inflamed more strongly with the fervor of charity"(4LAg 27).[30] We humans are loved so much that God in Christ chose to come to be one with us in our humanity. Like the beloved of a human lover, we can only respond appropriately by receiving God's love, allowing it to penetrate our very being and expressing love to God and others in return.

Indeed, being so touched by love is a life-changing experience. When people are "in love" they act differently–they smile more, they have a twinkle in their eyes, they are more positive and generous toward others. It was the goal of Clare and the Poor Ladies to become as loving and as generous as Christ Incarnate. This was their way of living out the reality of the Incarnation.

The Passion and Human Dignity

For Clare, perhaps the most persuasive dimension of Christ's poverty was his passion. In fact, the image of the suffering Christ stands at the center of the four-part process for prayer that Clare recommends to Agnes of Prague:

> Your Spouse, *though more beautiful than the children of men* (Ps. 44:33), became, for your salvation, the lowest of men, was despised, struck, scourged untold times throughout His entire body, and then died amid the suffering of the Cross.
>
> O most noble Queen,
> gaze upon [Him],
> consider [Him],
> contemplate [Him],
> as you desire to imitate [Him].
> If you suffer with him, *you will reign with Him.*
> [If you] weep [with Him], you shall rejoice with Him;
> [If you] die with Him on the cross of tribulation, you shall possess heavenly mansions *in the splendor of the saints* and, *in the Book of Life,* your *name* shall be called glorious among men (2LAg 20-22).[31]

Through contemplative prayer, in loving meditation on Christ's passion, people can be affirmed in their dignity and worth and changed for a lifetime. In human growth and development, a child is confirmed in her dignity and worth when she begins to understand the love of a parent, whom, she observes, works two jobs late into the night to support the family and yet never fails to get up early each morning to pack lunches for school and cook breakfast. In a similar way, people can confirm and solidify their knowledge of their own dignity through contemplation of the passion of Christ. Through empathetic "co-suffering" with Christ, we can come to know the deep abiding love of God for us and be moved to love others in a like manner.

Eucharist and Human Dignity

In a time when it was not customary to do so, Clare received the Eucharist frequently.[32] Indeed, Clare's great reverence for the Eucharist was demonstrated not only in her frequent reception of the sacrament but also in how she treated items associated with it. Even when seriously ill, Clare made fine linen corporals for use in the churches in the region of Assisi. She had special boxes lined in purple silk (the fabric traditionally used to make royal garments) in which to pack the corporals that were taken, often by friars, to the churches that needed them.

Perhaps the best-known example of Clare's understanding of the power of the real presence of Christ in the Eucharist is found in the narrative of her fending off the Saracens who broke into San Damiano, intent on destroying the town of Assisi. When Clare heard that the Saracens had entered the monastery, she asked for the small box in which the Blessed Sacrament of the Body of our Lord Jesus Christ was reserved. Clare then prayed, asking God to protect her sisters because she herself was powerless to do so.[33] Others describing that same incident also stressed that Clare asked the entire community to pray with her, and their prayers were answered. The Saracens departed, leaving both the Poor Ladies and the town unharmed.[34] Clearly, there was little doubt in Clare's mind that the One who loved so much that He humbled Himself to be present in the Eucharistic bread would also preserve the dignity of the Poor Ladies and her beloved home of Assisi.

Clare required all who joined the Poor Ladies to believe in the real presence of Christ in the Eucharist, as the Church taught.[35] Clare showed her value for the Eucharist by making special mention of it in her Rule. She made exceptions for chaplains to enter the cloister to celebrate the Eucharist for both the sick sisters and those who were well.[36] And at a time when frequent reception of the Eucharist was the exception rather than the rule, she included the requirement that the Poor Ladies receive communion at least seven times a year.[37] It is not difficult to conclude that, as a Catholic and as a lover of the poor Christ, Clare knew the marvelous loving presence of Christ in the Eucharist. There she experienced a powerful affirmation of her dignity.

Perhaps we can begin to grasp what it might have been like for her, if we reflect on how we feel when we are with our best friend or with someone we know loves us. In such situations, it is not difficult to return love and become changed in the process. Therein lies the secret of the Eucharist and human dignity for Clare and for us. Once we know our own dignity through the eyes of another, we are in-spired and empowered to pass on the experience to others.

Human Dignity Embodied:
Following in the Footprints of Jesus

Beyond any doubt, Jesus was the model for both Francis and Clare, the one whom they were determined to follow. In fact, Clare com-mended Agnes of Prague for doing just that: "As someone zealous for the holiest of poverty, in the spirit of great humility and the most ardent charity, you have held fast *to the footprints* (1 Pt. 2:22) of Him to Whom you have merited to be joined as a Spouse"(2LAg 7).[38] Though Clare did not use the phrase as Francis did, she certainly followed Jesus in every way and saw imitation of Him as her life's work.[39] Indeed, the reality of Clare's imitation of Christ was so ap-parent that it was used by Innocent IV as a reason for giving ap-proval to Clare's *Form of Life* (Rule):

> Because you have rejected the splendors and pleasures of the world and, following in the footprints of Christ Himself (cf. 1 Pt. 2:21) and His Most Holy Mother, you have chosen to live bodily enclosed and to serve the Lord in the highest poverty that, in freedom of soul, you may be the Lord's ser-vants (RCl 2).[40]

We can conclude from this that something was going on in Clare's life that spoke to others about Christ.

Certainly Clare's way of making human dignity concrete in-volved contemplation, silent suffering, the practice of spiritual pov-erty, living simply as the poor, and communal charity. However, we know that San Damiano was not hermetically sealed off from the world. There are numerous stories of how Clare and the Poor La-dies received the poor and the suffering of the region and assisted them both spiritually and with the basic necessities of life. In fact, Clare was known for her gift of healing. For example, an insane brother, a young boy with a pebble stuck in his nose, a young boy with a fever, a child with a film on his eye were all healed by her.[41] Clare's form of life was unique in that there was so much interac-tion with the world outside the monastery enclosure.

No doubt Clare understood her vocation not only as a personal love affair with God, but as a life lived for the sake of the Church and, indeed, for the whole world. She writes in her Third Letter to Agnes of Prague: "I consider you a co-worker of God Himself (cf. 1 Cor. 3:9; Rom. 16:3) and a support of the weak members of His ineffable Body"(3LAg 8).[42] The dignity that Clare and the Poor ladies realized in their life of contemplative prayer clearly was made concrete in many ways beyond the wall of the enclosure.

In this regard, Clare and her sisters provide a superb model for a genuinely respectful human way of life. They exhibit an important starting point for such living, namely, a sense of self that is secured in a true understanding of the virtue of humility.[43] Rooted in the love of God, their relationships went beyond mere acquaintances or business-like associations. Elizabeth A. Dreyer points out that the sisters' relationships were marked by true affectionate friendship.[44] Not only were their ties friendly and rooted in humility, they were distinctively mutual. As Margaret Carney sees it, there were three aspects to this mutual charity: "(1) individual sisters in their activity contribute to a loving environment; (2) the abbess and other officials of the community have specific responsibilities to foster charity; (3) the structures and norms of the community contribute to the basic justice that makes charity possible."[45]

Human dignity was embodied in meeting psychosocial needs and forgiveness among the sisters. Through little everyday practices and attitudes, the value of human life was exhibited. With an amazingly modern sensitivity to the kinds of conditions necessary to support a wholesome quality of human life, Clare, in her *Rule*, set up a way of life that reflected great reverence and respect for human life. For example, Chapter 5:4 says: "[The sisters] can communicate always and everywhere, briefly and in a low tone of voice, whatever necessary." This is a simple recognition that "touching base" with someone can provide a sense of personal worth and belonging. No human person can live long in isolation. On the other hand, if the sisters engage in gossip or if there is any kind of injury done to one sister by another, the one who caused the problem must,

> before offering her gift of prayer to the Lord, not only prostrate herself humbly at once at the feet of the other and ask pardon, but also beg her to intercede for her to the Lord that

He might forgive her. Let the other sister, mindful of that word of the Lord: "If you do not forgive from the heart, neither will your heavenly Father forgive you," generously pardon her sister every wrong she has done her (RCl 9:6-10).[46]

The generosity modeled by this kind of forgiveness is nothing other than God's great love for every human person. Greater regard for the human person will never be found!

Clare governed the community using structures of shared authority. Though given the canonical title of "Abbess," she never used it for self-aggrandizement, and she rarely exercised the full power over the sisters that the office technically provided. According to her *Rule*, the Abbess was to be chosen by common consent.[47] The Abbess was to "call weekly chapters," "publicly confess her offenses" and "preserve unity and mutual love and peace"(RCl 4:15-16, 22).[48] Inclusive and participative language is used throughout Clare's writings, including references to "our way of life," "our rule," or "our profession." One might say that Clare chose to exercise her power *with* her sisters, rather than *over* them. In fact, she made provisions in her *Rule* for the Poor Ladies to participate fully in the governance of the community.[49] Clearly, Clare valued mutuality.

Though Clare and the Poor Ladies exercised physical disciplines, they maintained respect for the human body. Clare's sense of human dignity required equal regard for all people. She did not neglect the particularities of relating to all her sisters according to the requirements of each one's distinct personality or bodily needs. It is well known that, in Clare's time, women's bodies were considered evil and weak, and therefore women often engaged in severe fasting and other harsh physical disciplines. There is evidence that some considered Clare's discipline of poverty too harsh and tried to get her to change her *Form of Life*.[50] However, according to Ingrid J. Peterson:

Neither Clare of Assisi nor the women who testified about her told of the need to do external penance because women's flesh was evil. In her *Third Letter to Agnes*, while Clare acknowledged that the flesh is weak, it is precisely the reason Clare urged Agnes not to be so severe in fasting.[51]

In fact, Clare regarded the body of the Virgin Mary as the throne of God on earth since she brought Jesus, the Son of God, into the world.[52] To Clare's mind, this reality assures her of the dignity of the human body as the dwelling place for God on earth.

Further, Clare's letters to Agnes of Prague are full of images, accessible only through human sensation, that describe the wonder, power, and beauty of contemplation and union with God. One sample will serve our purpose:

> Happy, indeed, is she to whom it is given to share in this sacred banquet so that she might cling with all her heart to [Christ] Whose beauty all the blessed hosts of heaven unceasingly admire, Whose affection excites, Whose contemplation refreshes, Whose kindness fulfills, Whose delight replenishes, Whose remembrance delightfully shines, by Whose fragrance the dead are revived, Whose glorious vision will bless all the citizens of the heavenly Jerusalem, which since it is the splendor of eternal glory is the brilliance of eternal light and the mirror without blemish (4LAg 9-14).[53]

The human body is part of what makes each person unique and able to experience the many ways God is revealed to us. Clare viewed moderate fasting as a constructive discipline, but abuse of the body was not a necessary condition to receive God's love. In fact, Clare regularly exempted the younger and the sick sisters, as well as those who worked outside the monastery from fasting.[54] The human body is good and valuable, and our human dignity requires that we care for our physical selves.

The relationship between Francis and Clare was one of equality and mutual respect. Theirs was not a romantic bond, but rather a deep spiritual friendship nurtured through a common desire for God and a passion for life. Together, they established new ways of living the Gospel. While there was a risk that their activities would be read by others with suspicion, perceived as scandalous, or even judged heretical, they shared and nurtured one another through teaching, prayer, discernment, sufferings and successes.[55] Throughout, however, they each maintained their distinct personhood and style of life. It is important to note that both considered the vocation and the rights of the sisters to be equal with those of the brothers.[56]

In addition to her loving deference towards her sisters, Clare continued to nurture relationships with the Friars Minor. After Francis's death, these relationships became strained. Rather than abandon them, Clare, rooted in the love of God, continued to draw upon Francis's pledge to her and her sisters that the friars would care for them with love and solicitude. Clare and the Poor Ladies, on their part, continued to extend loving care and solicitude to the friars.

Human Dignity and Human Creaturehood

Completely confident in the deep and abiding love of God for herself and for all others created in God's image and likeness, Clare shows us that such self-understanding "frees one to respect and raise up the 'other'–whether the other be a person or a tree or a paper wasp–as also made and loved by God."[57] Certainly Clare did not consider the world an evil place. However, in her fervor to live in God's presence and contemplate Christ, she saw the world as a potential distraction from her focus on Christ. She saw the created world–apart from humans–limited in its potential to contain the Creator as could the human soul. While she understood God as the one source of fulfillment and security, by contrast the world is momentary and filled with distractions and temptations. Yet, she saw herself and the Poor Ladies as creatures dependent on God like the "lilies of the field" and "the birds of the air," cared for equally well by the same loving God. This attitude freed her to appreciate the beauty of creation and her relationship to it without being deterred by it. Thus, Clare and Francis were like-minded, praising God *through* creatures, not *in* them nor identifying God with them.

Embracing Bodily Death as Part of Human Life

Clare died as she had lived–surrounded by her sisters and in prayer. When she wrote her last letter to Agnes of Prague, she was aware that the end was near: "Farewell, my dearest daughter, to you and to your daughters until we meet at the throne of the glory of the great God" (4LAg 39).[58] This is a hopeful statement that speaks of ultimate fulfillment. Clare achieved many things during her lifetime. Perhaps the greatest of them all was establishing a way of life that fully imitated the poor Christ. She hoped that, before her death, she might receive official Church approval of the *Form of Life* (Rule) and the final blessing for her Privilege of Poverty. That, indeed, happened.[59]

There is no doubt that Clare understood death as the pathway to the fulfillment of her life's quest for an intimate relationship with God in Christ. She laid claim to nothing beyond that profound desire. She died embraced by love and fully free. What is perhaps most touching concerning her death and revealing of "the human" is that she encouraged her soul on its way home to heaven like a mother assures a child: "Go calmly and in peace, for you will have a good escort, because He Who created you has sent you the Holy Spirit and has always guarded you as a mother does her child who loves her. . . . O Lord, may You Who created me, be blessed" (Proc 3:20).[60] Would that each of us might die with such awareness of God's love and embrace.

Thus, we catch a glimpse of how Lady Clare and the Poor Ladies contributed to a Franciscan theology of the human. In our world where the predominant paradigm of relationship is dominance and oppression of the less powerful by the more powerful, both human and non-human, Clare shows a way of engaged and respectful human living. Beginning with the self confidence of one beloved of God (who even cares for the birds of the air and the lilies of the field) and with a respectful courtly bow to all of creation, Clare shows us a life marked by true deference, love and equal regard for others, the fruits of which are sensitivity, unity and harmony. It is this kind of human living that marks the paradigm to which our civilization must shift if, indeed, our planet is to survive.[61] By being mutually attuned to the "other," we can achieve the security of life and relationship that is often the goal of those who wield wealth and power, but which often eludes them.

SUMMARY:
LESSONS FROM FRANCIS AND CLARE

What can we learn from Francis and Clare that shapes a Franciscan understanding of the human person? What, in practical terms, does it mean to say that humans are deified by the Incarnation, redeemed through the Passion and nurtured by the Eucharist? What difference does this make to ordinary persons in their daily life?

1. Humans have an inviolable dignity because God created each person through love and for love. As scripture tells us, each human being bears God's very image and likeness (Gen. 1:26). This means that humans are whole persons, distinct from the other creatures that were created "each after their own kind" (Gen. 1:24). Each person is unique, yet joined to all others in a common humanness. Humans retain God's image in spite of being born into a world where each is affected by more sin than he or she actually commits and even though each personally sins. Overwhelmingly, God's generous love abounds and human beings, in the face of sin, are continually called to the very heart of God. They are also given the responsibility of being co-creators and co-redeemers with God, using their gifts and talents for the common good of all creation, but especially for the poor. They are enjoined to treat all other human beings with reverence and respect out of deference to the divine image. All women and men bear this divine image equally, so this rules out any forms of racism, sexism and the like.

2. Human existence is deified by the Incarnation. Jesus Christ, the Son of God, became one like us, a physical-and-spiritual being. In God's wisdom, God chose to express boundless love in a way humans could grasp best, specifically in the person of Jesus. This action of God reaffirmed the goodness of humanity. Also, Jesus is the model for what true humanity needs to be. Our way to wholeness and holiness is to become like Christ–fully human– developing our God-given gifts and talents as completely as we can and sharing them with others.

3. In their writings, as well as by the way they lived, Francis and Clare, confirmed the goodness of the human body. Yet neither saint came to that positive stance without a struggle. Indeed, the effort to see bodily goodness was an important part of each one's journey of conversion. In today's world, there are all kinds of physical abuse: there is abuse in families; there is prostitution; there is drug abuse by athletes and others; there is pornography, slavery, torture; there is obsession with physical beauty and fixation on body weight. The views of Francis and Clare challenge such a status quo. By contrast, they stress the goodness of the body and reverence for it. All bodies are good. Women's bodies are not sources of evil, as many have believed for centuries. Indeed, it was through a human body (Mary's) and with a human body (Jesus') that God entered our world. Through our bodies—for good or for ill—we touch people and enter into relationships with them. We experience union with Christ bodily as we receive the Eucharistic bread and wine. It is through the "human touch" of our loved ones that we know analogously what the love of God is like. It follows then that our humanness requires us to extend a healing touch to the "untouchables" of our time and place, because Christ fully embraced us, becoming flesh for us.

4. To see any value in pain and suffering, we must experience it with new eyes. Certainly, as Francis and Clare eventually realized, we need not search out suffering in our world—there is suffering aplenty! But fidelity to learning from life's hurts is a fight worth waging. Indeed, because we know what physical pain and suffering are like, we can realize the depth and breadth of God's deep love for us in the passion. It is this wondrous and boundless love that compels us to conversion of heart, actions of love and justice and contemplation of the One who draws us close. Our human senses and emotions are valuable and good, alerting us to the deepest complexities of our existence and enabling us to respond to others with sensitivity and kindness.

5. Following Jesus' example, as one who emptied himself of godly power and prestige (Phil. 4:1-11), humans are at their best when they surrender themselves to God's love and care. Ironically, it

is then that we are most powerful and most free. It is then that the power of love is ours to use in the service of others, especially the poor. We become transformed, concerned about establishing mutual relationships, rather than "lording it over" others. In fact, with this Christ-like attitude, there are no "others"; there are no "enemies." Rather there are only companions on the journey to God. When we live in such a God-infused world, there is very little that really threatens us. As Francis so clearly showed us, all the little "deaths," in which we struggle with disappointments, our own limitations, or the limitations of others, and even "Sister Death" herself, cannot separate us from the love of God. As Clare showed, what separates us from God and our fellow humans is our clinging to a poor self-image, being egotistical, failing to seek forgiveness or refusing to generously forgive someone else.

DISCUSSION QUESTIONS

1. In an age of terrorism, torture, and genocide, is it possible to do anything to regain a sense of human dignity and to shift the flow of world events? What might we do alone? With others?

2. What insights from Francis might be helpful for a healthy understanding of death in today's world?

3. Do we have any "others" or "enemies" in our life? How might we begin to "love" them? How does our daily life show how we value our physical bodies? Are there changes we could make in order to value our bodies as God values them? What might we do to assist our sisters and brothers to be more loving towards their bodies?

PART THREE
HUMANS–MEDIATORS OF GOD:

SOME CENTRAL ELEMENTS IN
ST. BONAVENTURE OF BAGNOREGIO

INTRODUCTION

Without St. Francis of Assisi, there would be no St. Bonaventure, as we know him today. The influence of Francis and Clare on Bonaventure is seen primarily in the way his theology begins and ends with the person of Christ. Bonaventure applied a more sophisticated and intellectual method of theological reflection and interpretation to Francis's intuitive approach to Christ and to his mystical religious experience.[62] Bonaventure, for example, follows Francis, who frequently names God the "Supreme Good." But Bonaventure uses the philosophical Pseudo-Dionysian notion *Bonum est diffusivum sui*[63]–Goodness is self-diffusive. He calls God *"fontalis plenitudo,"*(Font of All Goodness). Bonaventure tries to convey the basic idea that, just as someone is full of excitement about a good thing that has happened and simply *needs to share* the news with another, so too, God is so full of goodness that it simply *overflows in the divine creativity* that brings the universe into existence. Bonaventure, the Seraphic Doctor, gave the spirituality of the Little Poor Man of Assisi a philosophical and theological framework.

In this section, then, we uncover Bonaventure's contributions to a Franciscan view of the human person. We describe some of the philosophical concepts Bonaventure uses to explain his understanding of the human person and some of the significant characteristics he posits about the human person. The insights of Bonaventure recorded in the thirteenth century still serve to deepen our understanding of humans as creatures connected to all creation and as persons bonded to God.

31

ST. BONAVENTURE'S THOUGHT: TRINITARIAN STRUCTURE, IMAGINATION AND METAPHYSICS

In Bonaventure's work we find grounds, not only for the sacredness of creation in general, but for the value of each element in particular, including each human person. In order to understand Bonaventure, one must be aware of the many dimensions of his thought and the two kinds of language he employs.[64] He uses both the language of the imagination and the language of metaphysics.[65] It is important to note that Bonaventure sees the imagination and metaphysics as interconnected and he understands that they impact one another. As Zachary Hayes shows, at the core of Bonaventure's theology is the doctrine of the Trinity.[66]

Bonaventure understands the Trinity as divine exemplarity: that is, the immense fecundity (productiveness) of the goodness of God expressed in the emanation (giving out) of the Three Persons and flowing outward into the created cosmos. More precisely, from the fecundity of the First Person of the Trinity (Father), there emanates the Word (Second Person) *and* spirates the Holy Spirit of Love (Third Person).[67] (The alert reader will notice how this structure permeates the thought of the Seraphic Doctor; that is, he seems to see the world in threes.)

At the level of the imagination, the world outside ourselves impacts our consciousness through our senses–touch, taste, smell, hearing and sight–and we make judgments about what we experience. Bonaventure held that, because God created all things, we could know something about God by experiencing the created world.[68]

However, our intellect is also involved in knowing. As we reflect on the information given us by our senses, we raise the metaphysical questions of interpretation and meaning. We move to the ontological[69] level of finding the nature of God reflected in the encounters brought by the senses. Here we see Bonaventure use the Platonic philosophical tradition to show that the nature of the created order is conditioned by the nature of the Creator, and all created reality is grounded in God. In light of this understanding of Bonaventure's thought, we now examine more closely human creaturehood and human identity.

THE HUMAN PERSON IN THE CREATED WORLD: EXEMPLARITY AND LOVE

Bonaventure explains the existence of the created world as the result of the tremendous fruitfulness of the goodness of God. As Hayes shows, Bonaventure addresses divine exemplarity by building on Pseudo-Dionysius's Neo-Platonic principle that goodness is necessarily self-diffusive and on the Victorine understanding of ecstatic love.[70] Exemplarity for Bonaventure expresses the fundamental claim that all created reality is grounded in God and therefore manifests something of the mysteries of God in the created world. The nature of the created order is conditioned by the nature of the Creator. The triune God expresses a productive love within the Godhead that is the emanation (giving out or expression) of the Three Persons. The divine life of the Godhead flows outward and is reflected in the created cosmos. The entire created world is therefore *theophanic*–it images God in varying degrees.[71]

Humans: *Similitude* of God among Creatures

All living things are vestiges (resemblances) of God. However, humans represent God most closely and distinctly because, as Scripture tells us, they were created in God's very image and likeness (Gen. 1:26). Humans can be most thoroughly influenced by God's goodness and grace and can become a *similitude* (visible likeness) representing God most closely.[72] Divine exemplarity culminates in the figure of Christ–the Incarnation of the Divine Word, the Art of the Father, in which the divine exemplarity is most concentrated. In the conjunction of the divine archetype and the microcosm of creation, creation is transformed and fulfilled in union with God.[73]

> So, when the divine exemplarity is focused so sharply in the self-expressive Word; when that Word enters into the most profound relationship to creation in the humanity of Jesus, this conjunction of the divine archetype and what Bonaventure calls the microcosm (because something of all creation is in human nature) when that comes together, this is the synthesis of all that makes up the created cosmos. It is

at that conjunction when the divine aim for all creation is brought to fruition.[74]

Humans: Loved, Not Lost

According to Bonaventure, that is why God created–so that through love, the creation can be brought into a kind of transforming fullness in union with the divine.[75] And that happens first and to the fullest extent in Jesus. Given this vision, we can say that the world of creation has its own truth, goodness and beauty.[76] However, there is much more to this story. "Beyond this, each creature in itself and all creation is in its truest reality an expressive sign of the glory, truth, and beauty of God. Only when it is seen in these terms is it seen in its most profound significance."[77] Here is the basis upon which we can hold that each element of creation has intrinsic value in itself.

Bonaventure's metaphysics grounds a whole series of metaphors revelatory of the cosmos and expressive of his understanding of creation. The Seraphic Doctor employed metaphorical language to show the relationship between God and the cosmos. Hayes summarizes Bonaventure's vision of the world of creation, given at the level of metaphor and symbol, in this way:

> [F]or Bonaventure, the relationship between creation and God can be expressed in two words–manifestation and participation. All things in the cosmos exist so as to manifest something of the mystery of God. And all things exist by virtue of some degree of participation in the mystery of being that flows from the absolute mystery of the creative love of God. An appropriate reading of the book of the cosmos, therefore, gives us some sense of the divine goodness and fecundity; of the divine wisdom and beauty; of the divine intelligence and freedom; and of the relational character of the divine mystery of the trinity in which all of creation is grounded. It gives us some sense of the pain and tragedy of existence in a fallen condition.[78]

Though after the fall (Gen. 3) the human view of God's self-revelation in creation was obscured, it was not lost. Biblical and historical revelation supplement and clarify what we see in nature and enable us to read the cosmic revelation with greater accuracy. The story of the love of God expressed in creation is elaborated in the Scriptures and modeled most perfectly in the person, life and ministry of Jesus. In the end, there is little excuse for those who do not heed the call to return to the Fountain Source of all Goodness, as Bonaventure exhorts:

> Open your eyes, alert your spiritual ears, unseal your lips, and apply your heart so that in all creatures you may see, hear, praise, love, serve, glorify and honor God, lest the whole world rise up against you. For the "universe shall wage war against the foolish." On the contrary, it will be a matter of glory for the wise who can say with the prophet: "For you have given me O Lord, a delight in your deeds, and I will rejoice in the work of your hands. How great are your works, O Lord! You have made all things in wisdom. The earth is filled with your creatures."[79]

Humans: Dignity of the Image of God Explained

At the very heart of Bonaventure's understanding of the human person is the belief that humans are created in the image of God, as confirmed in Scripture (Gen. 1:26). The Seraphic Doctor goes to some length to explain how that is possible and what it means. According to Bonaventure, humans, unlike other creatures, are created with the power to know divine goodness both through the material world (mediately) and directly (immediately) like spiritual beings. The human soul is a body-spirit (not dualistic) relationship. For example: the soul has the capacity to physically "see" a dog with the eye of the body. But it also has the spiritual ability to understand that the dog is an animal, to desire to play or communicate with it, to comprehend it as a creature created by God and to recognize that it reveals something about what God is like. Humans bear some similarity to God in that the human soul (the very essence of life) is a body-spirit relationship that reflects the power, wisdom and goodness of God.

Human Soul: Power to Conceive of the Divine

The powers of the soul are memory, intellect and will.[80] The memory includes the capability of recalling the past. But, in Bonaventure's use of this term, memory also comprises our awareness of the present and our ability to anticipate the future. In addition, the memory holds the most foundational notions concerning how the world is put together and what God is like.

The intellect is that power of the soul that engages our cognitive functions. It is where we reason things out logically, bring our ideas to expression in language, think of new ideas and come to judgments about the being of things. In Bonaventure's perception, it is this power of the soul that can conceive of the possibility of absolute being, or God. God illuminates the human intellect; that is, God enables us to know things with certainty that we cannot account for logically, but can know only through natural intuition or in the light of faith (revealed in Scripture, Tradition and prayerful contemplation).

The will is the soul's power to desire, deliberate and make judgments about the good (i.e., about morality—what is right or wrong, good or bad). Bonaventure understands that it is from this power of the soul that the human heart desires the highest good, namely, God. As Bonaventure understands it, both the intellect and the will "indicate a close relationship between the human soul and the reality of God as supreme truth and goodness."[81]

Human Body: A Beautiful Matter

As Bonaventure sees it, the human body is connected to the soul and governed by it. But Bonaventure does not demean the body. On the contrary, as Ilia Delio explains, Bonaventure proclaims that the body "is the noblest constitution and organization that exists in nature, possessing the 'greatest variety of organs, endowed with the greatest beauty and skill and manageableness.'"[82] So the body is a beautiful thing that enjoys the guidance of the soul. In a magnificent orderly way, God directs the soul by illumination and the body through free will. Thus, while the body and all bodily functions are subject to the spirit, the spirit is subject to God. Indeed, the human person is a union of spirit and matter. As such, the human is in the perfect position—the middle—to be the vital link between the two extremes of creation. Bonaventure considers the human as both the completion and the consummation of God's work of creation:

Because the first principle was the most powerful, wise, and good in production, and because [God] has made this manifest in all his effects in a certain way, he ought to manifest this most impressively in his last and most noble effect. Such is man, whom he produced last among the creatures so that in man he should appear most potently, and the accomplishment of the divine works should be reflected in him.[83]

Because the soul is united with the body, humans are joined to the material world. It is necessary for humans to use the material world to express themselves and to maintain a balanced harmonious relationship between God, themselves and all creation.

HUMAN IDENTITY: IMAGE OF GOD AND IMAGE OF CHRIST

Image of God

Humans, who image God, are also bearers of God (*capax Dei*). Humans are capable of becoming God-like, participating in life with God, actually receiving God into their being.[84] The very way God made humans sets them in position to discover truth and embrace goodness by using their God-given abilities of intellect and will. The human's physical body is significant for this discovery, as well. According to Bonaventure, we find truth and accept goodness first through the visible world of creation and everyday life (body); then, through the interior world of human consciousness, participating in the gift of God's grace; and ultimately, through contemplation in spiritual union with God (spirit). It is in the process of discovering truth and goodness that humans also find their own true identity. In his spiritual work, *Itinerarium Mentis in Deum* (*The Soul's Journey into God*), Bonaventure describes the process by which humans are conformed to God and become their truest selves. It is through opening oneself ever more completely to God's generous, overflowing love and grace that humans find their real identity and vocation.

Image of Christ

But humans are not made in the image of God in a general way. They are specifically made to the likeness of the Son who is both human and divine.[85] Ilia Delio explains:

> When the Word becomes flesh in the Incarnation, the truly human image of the divine is expressed in the person of Jesus Christ. As image of God, therefore, Christ not only reveals God to us but he reveals who we are in relation to God, that is the truth of our humanity.[86]

So it is we humans who are ordained to Christ, not Christ to us. This reality was important to Bonaventure in explaining the true nature of human persons. God loved humans so much as to humble himself and become one of us. Thus, because humans are made like God as most fully expressed (exemplarity) in Christ incarnate (Word), the very nature of human beings is to be like Christ–poor and humble–in relationship to God. Human existence is thus both limited and deified. The more we conform ourselves to Christ and the more we live into the reality of both aspects of our existence, the more fully human we become and the more God's life can shine through us. Bonaventure summed all of this up when he proclaimed: "I will see myself better in God than in myself."[87]

Mediators between God and Creation:
Humans in the Middle

Just as Christ, the second person of the Trinity is "in the middle" in relationship to the Father and the Spirit, so too, in Bonaventure's understanding, humans are situated in the middle of creation between the simply material beings (rocks, plants, animals) and the exclusively spiritual beings (angels). In keeping with the medieval scholastic way of explaining the world, Bonaventure held that reality was made up of both "matter" and "form." Form defines how something is conceptualized, how it appears, or how it is named. Matter defines the physical or material substance in which something takes shape. Bonaventure reasons that because humans are created as the most perfectly interrelated combination of form and matter, that is, because they are body-spirit beings, humans stand at the center of creation.[88]

Bonaventure saw humanity as God's greatest work. In the Genesis account of creation, humans are created last, and with that, God said it was "very good!" (Gen. 1:31). In the middle position, humans are the focus of creation. All other elements, plants and animals of the cosmos are given to humans for their use and care (Gen. 1: 28-30). Clearly, Bonaventure did not understand this middle position as giving humans license to abuse and "lord it over" the rest of creation. Rather, it is through exercising their powers of intellect, memory and will that humans find their role as *mediators* between God and creation and as guardians of the multiple manifestations of God's self-revelation.[89]

Freedom: Given and Gone Awry

Just as an artist knows what she intends a work of art to express, so too, God knows the potential of each human person. The artist also realizes that each person who experiences a work of art experiences it differently and thus she lets the work freely speak for itself. God, too, creates humans in freedom. Human freedom, according to Bonaventure, is both a blessing and the very thing that made the fall into sin possible. Bonaventure insists that there was a time when humans, created in the image of God with the capacity to relate to both the material world and to the divine, stood at the center of creation, contemplating and praising God. But then they became "entangled in an infinity of questions"–overstepping their true and proper role in creation.[90] Humans wanted to be like the Son. But instead of humbly turning to Christ, humans "turned away from the good and toward creatures, investing in others the goodness and truth that rightly belongs to God."[91] In turning away from God, humans broke their love relationship with the divine; they sinned.

Bonaventure clearly recognized two consequences of sin–personal and universal. At the personal level, there is a distortion of the image of God; that is, the person becomes unfocused, fragmented and muddled. One might say that personal sin involves humans operating with a false consciousness, depending on themselves and their own accumulation of knowledge, power and prestige for security, rather than trusting in God's boundless love and grace. The reality of humanity is that people are utterly dependent on God. This dependence on God's love and grace was the condition of original justice and peace that existed at the beginning of time.

According to Bonaventure, original sin resulted in the loss of grace and the whole of humanity was corrupted.[92] When Bonaventure speaks of this universal consequence of sin, he talks about a sundering of the unity of body and soul that existed in the original creation. So sin breaks up the order and harmony of the world, pitting humans against one another, against the created world and even against God. But that is not the end of Bonaventure's story.

Humans Return through the Passion of Christ Incarnate

In goodness and love, God intervened and, through the passion of Christ, humans were offered a path to return to God's loving embrace. Ilia Delio explains the beautiful analogy of a circle that Bonaventure used to illustrate this return to relationship with God:

> A center, he claims, maintains the perfect circle of emanation and reduction [leading back]. However, with sin, this center is lost due to the fall of "Adam." The center can only be restored when two lines intersect at right angles; thus it is Christ crucified who becomes the center and restores the circle of life to its perfect loving relationship with God.[93]

Bonaventure holds that it is solely through Jesus Christ, the Word made flesh, that humans escape their alienation and come home to God. Through the incarnate Christ (the human being who represents and contains in himself the entire natural created order), we come to know again the truth of all reality as we imitate Christ, the Word and Wisdom of God. As we interact with, study and meditate on the person, life, ministry, teachings and actions of Jesus, and especially his Passion, and probe the depths of their meaning for our lives, we find our way back to a renewed and restored relationship with God.

Remarkably, God takes the initiative to provide sanctifying grace to transform the intellect, memory and will such that the *similitude* of God can, once again, shine forth in each person. Throughout our life journey, this transformation continues until at life's end we receive our ultimate fulfillment in *deiformitas*—"an infusion of sanctifying grace that disposes one to find total fulfillment in the continuous act of loving God."[94] As Bonaventure so beautifully puts it:

> Hence in man's reward that godliness of glory (*deiformitas*) is given him by which he is conformed to God, sees God clearly with his reason, loves God with his will, and retains him forever in his memory. Thus, the whole soul lives, the whole soul is richly endowed with its three powers, the whole soul is joined to God, is united with him and rests in him, finding in him all good, peace, light, and eternal sufficiency. Hence, situated, "in the state of all good in a perfect gathering" and achieving eternal life, man is said to be happy and glorious.[95]

The final fulfillment of the human journey comes in the Resurrection, when the body and soul are reunited, achieving their fullness of perfection in God. In Bonaventure's understanding, in the final mediating act, humans represent the whole creation before God because the human body is the microcosm of the entire cosmos. In the Resurrection all created things will find their fulfillment through humankind insofar as humans are like every creature.

SUMMARY:
LESSONS FROM ST. BONAVENTURE OF BAGNOREGIO

Admittedly there are some aspects of Bonaventure's thought that can be troubling for the present day reader. He uses hierarchical notions in his metaphysics and his social thought. But if we can keep these aspects in perspective, knowing that he wrote in the thirteenth century, there is much that can be gleaned that is relevant for our day.

Naturally, because he built on the ideas of Francis and Clare, there is much in common between Bonaventure's ideas and those of the two saints of Assisi. Yet, often it is not an idea as such, but how an idea is stated or expressed that can open a new insight for us, advancing our perception and enabling us to comprehend something more deeply and thoroughly. Here are several insights from Bonaventure that develop the thought and spiritual insights of Francis and Clare.

1. Bonaventure clearly places humans in an intimate relationship
    with the created world. Yet each person has distinct characteris-
    tics that enable him/her to function differently from other crea-
    tures. However, human distinctiveness does not separate humans
    from the created order. In fact, the uniqueness of humans allows
    and requires them to respond to God in a particular way, namely,
    to mediate between God and all other creatures. Humans are to
    be advocates for other creatures, giving them voice before God
    and the world. On the other hand, other creatures inspire and
    thrill humans, arousing their awareness of the magnificence of
    God and inspiring contemplation. Certainly, in our ecologically
    threatened world, humans are also called to a profound rever-
    ence for one another and for the environment, since no human
    can live in an unhealthy milieu.

2. Humans are the *similitude* of God, the crown of creation. Cre-
    ated in the image and likeness of God, humans bear the greatest
    similarity to God. They are body-spirit creatures that know God
    and are known to God both innately and experientially. Human
    bodies are integral to human self-understanding and these bod-
    ies are good. Thus, there is no place for dualism in Bonaventure's
    notion of the human person. Both social and natural sciences in
    our day have demonstrated how intricately all aspects of the
    human person affect one another–social, physical, intellectual,
    emotional, etc. When the interrelationship of these aspects is
    neglected, whether in interpersonal relationships or in the struc-
    tures of societies, quality of life is diminished. In fact, dualistic
    ideas are at the root of many serious social, political and human
    rights issues, such as racism, ethnic superiority or sexism. Be-
    cause all humans bear God's image and likeness equally, dualis-
    tic claims of "superiority" or "inferiority," smack of false
    consciousness, false reality and sinfulness.

3. Certainly, the role of humans as persons "in the middle" dic-
    tates that the kind of power they choose to use needs to be "power
    with" others–supporting, encouraging and enabling–rather than
    "power over" others–intimidating, coercing or threatening. Be-
    cause true human identity is to be found in the imitation of Christ,
    human use of personal power and authority is necessarily modi-

fied. There is no place for arrogance in human interactions. Rather, humans need to join in humble service and mutual relationships, grounded in the reality that all of their gifts, talents and resources flow from God, the Fountain Source of All Goodness. As the poor Christ ministered to the poor and the outcast of his day, so too must humans serve others in their own time and place.

4. Because humans participate in the material world, they are historical beings. They grow, change and develop. Through their relationships with Christ, other humans, other earth creatures and through their reflection, they become increasingly more God-like and free. The more perfectly related people become, the more human they become. There is hope for humanity–room for repentance, reconciliation, renewal and restoration. Humans need only choose to stay open, attentive and engaged with God, with one another and with the entire created world.

QUESTIONS FOR DISCUSSION

1. Is there a dualistic attitude toward the human person (body/spirit) in our society? Racism? Sexism? Ethnic superiority?

2. As a human person "in the middle," how are you a mediator in daily life? At work? With friends? In relation to the created world?

PART FOUR
HUMANS–UNIQUELY GOD'S IN MUTUAL RELATIONSHIP

SOME CENTRAL ELEMENTS IN BL. JOHN DUNS SCOTUS

INTRODUCTION

John Duns Scotus is known as the "Subtle Doctor" for a reason. His thought frequently combined philosophical ideas and theological notions, integrating them to form a new understanding. Yet, he is a true son of St. Francis and St. Clare. At the heart of his thought stands a free, generous and loving God, who from the moment of creation delighted in the uniqueness of each human being. Duns Scotus sees God as the creative artist who affirms humanity from the beginning by envisioning the Incarnation, who accepts human goodness, and draws each person into the divine "Beatific Embrace."[96]

Throughout his work, Scotus is concerned to understand all reality as a whole, from both human and divine perspectives. No doubt his most important contribution to the Franciscan understanding of the human person is that he demonstrates how both the human and divine partners are able to choose a dynamic reciprocal relationship that leads to the optimal thriving of humanity, while protecting the ultimate freedom of God. The suggestion of a relationship, named by modern feminists as "mutuality,"[97] can be found in Scotus's metaphysical commitment to the *univocity of being*,[98] to the *essential order* and to his definition of moral goodness as the harmony of circumstances under the direction of right reason. These metaphysical constructs work in tandem with the paradigms of divine mutuality that he draws from divine revelation.

Scotus's metaphysical ideas are grounded in his perception of the nature of God, the divine essence that is expressed as person in the communion of the Trinity. Each person of the Trinity conveys

God's essence, but the three persons together reflect the divine in a way not possible for the single person. Divine revelation discloses several paradigmatic relationships between God and humankind that suggest mutuality. These are the life of the Trinity, the Incarnation, *imago Dei*, Covenant (Decalogue) and *acceptatio* in the order of merit.

HUMANS IN CONTEXT: CREATION AND THE CREATOR

Contingency and the Necessity of God

In order to understand how John Duns Scotus perceives humanity, we need first to understand his view of God's relationship to creation and the value he places on the created world in general and on the dignity of creation overall. Scotus began with empirical observation of the created world in its totality.

As a Christian, he realized that there was *nothing* that remained forever and that *everything* was ultimately dependent on God for its life and existence. He expressed this insight in the metaphysical notion of *contingency*, that is, the reality that things or situations do not have to exist *at all* nor do they need to exist *as* they exist; they *are utterly dependent on something or someone else* to bring them to life or make them happen. For example: A rose could be red, yellow or pink. If the gardener does not water the rosebush, it will die. The gardener might care for the rose so well that it wins a prize at a garden show. On the other hand, there is only so much the gardener can do to make the rose grow in a particular way; all else depends on its God-given capacity to live and grow.

Scotus reasoned that *if* something *exists* (a stone, for example), that means it is somehow *possible* for it to exist under the right conditions (lava from a volcano cooled into obsidian, for example). He traced backward through a series of causes that could make something exist or happen in order to reach the ultimate point of origin where a being existed that itself had no cause but yet had the potential to cause other things; and he ended up with *only* God. For Scotus, the only being that is not contingent, but uncaused and *necessary*, is God. God is *necessary* simply because there is *nothing* that could bring about God or "make God happen." The Divine Being exists because God chooses to exist, and creation exists because God artistically, freely and lovingly calls it into being in the act of creating it. That God is *love* was most important for Scotus, as it is for us.[99] Because God is absolutely free, God is absolutely loving; and this love is absolutely immanent (present, here with us). As long as anything exists, God is present to sustain it. This stands in contrast with the watchmaker model or machine model of the universe proposed by the Enlightenment philosophers or Deists of the past.

God Created to Make His Glory Known

Scotus explains the kind of power God has and discusses how that power was used to bring about creation. God's power is manifested in two manners: first, *potentia absoluta,* which allows God to act with indifference toward creation (i.e., not be influenced by it). This power might seem threatening and not typical of someone who loves. However, because God is always loving and rational, the exercise of divine power is always rational and never arbitrary.

Potentia ordinata refers to what God has actually chosen to do and has in fact done. It requires conformity to rules predetermined by divine wisdom or motivated by the divine will.[100] To be sure, things work the way God created them to work, and God respects the requirements of this world because they express the divine creative intent. This consistency in God and in God's actions serves as an affirmation of humanity in that it inspires trust, fidelity and orderliness, making possible a loving human-divine relationship.

Divine revelation and the accounts of salvation history witness to the fact that God is loving and faithful through all times and circumstances. So, in short, God chose to create to make his glory known (the ontological holiness of God; see Eph. 1:3-10). Such an utterly free God did not *have* to do anything. Indeed, the entire created world is pure grace and gift given out of love and to express love.

Haecceitas

There is another aspect of creation that is the focus of Scotus's attention and that profoundly reveals the great dignity of God's creation. The Subtle Doctor claims that in order for one subject to be related to another, it must *first* be known and understood for what it is *in itself*. Scotus's principle of *haecceitas*[101] (individuation or "thisness") provides the philosophical foundation for all created realities being specified (identified as specific entities). *Haecceitas* makes a singular thing what it is and differentiates it from all other things (of common nature) to which it may be compared (because of its commonality).[102]

For example: The principle of *haecceitas* holds that if I have a bouquet of flowers (items of a common nature) made up of a dozen roses and a dozen daisies, I have not only a bouquet (things of a common nature), roses (that can be compared because of their commonality) and daisies (that can be compared because of their commonality), but I have *twelve distinct individual flowers* that can be judged to be enough alike as to call them roses and *twelve distinct individual flowers* that can be judged to be enough alike as to call them daisies. In Scotus's thought, a rose is a rose and not a daisy; and each rose or each daisy is distinct from every other rose and every other daisy! So too it is with all of creation, including human beings. Each person is unique in all time and for all eternity–there never has been nor will there ever be another human being identical to you or to me; no, not even a clone! A human person's identity cannot be reduced to her or his physical make-up or current embodied existence. As Mary Beth Ingham so aptly puts it:

> Haecceitas points to the ineffable within each being. The sacredness of each person, indeed of each being is philosophically expressed in this Latin term. According to Scotus, the created order is not best understood as a transparent medium through which divine light shines (as Aquinas taught), but is itself endowed with an inner light that shines forth from within. The difference between these two great scholars can be compared to the difference between a window (Aquinas) and a lamp (Scotus). Both give light, but the source of light for Scotus has already been given to the being by the creator. Each being within the created order already possesses an immanent dignity; it is already gifted by the loving Creator with sanctity beyond our ability to understand.[103]

Not only does the entire creation have dignity because of its vastness and diversity; it is profoundly valuable because of its particularity–each being in itself. Thus, from the context of creation, Scotus uncovers a Creator, who is powerful, artistically free, loving and who sustains creation in general and in particular in an ordered and absolutely loving way. Most important for our purposes is that *haecceitas* makes each person distinct, one from the other. Without individuation, in which there are at least two distinct entities, no authentic interpersonal relationship is possible.

Relationships Made Possible:
The Essential Order and the Univocity of Being

Duns Scotus is what philosophers today would call a *moderate realist*[104]–he believed that human concepts have real existence. Just as a road map relates to the road by a one to one correspondence, so too there are links between our concepts and the world around us. This way of understanding the world is important, because it makes possible human thought, the capability of linking particularities (*haecceitas*) with a more general awareness of the world. It also makes it possible to move to conclusions that deepen human understanding. When thinking about the world or about a set of ideas, humans connect what certain objects or ideas have in common because of the very fact of their existence; namely, their common "being-ness" or *ens commune*.

Not only does reality share in being, but it also is created in an *essential order*. Everything in the universe connects to everything else in either a *prior* or *posterior* relationship. God as the *First Principle* is prior to all others and posterior to none. But this reality does not hinder the loving bond between God and creatures and especially humans. The very fact that God, humans and all other creatures of creation are intimately linked at the level of *being* enables relationships to come about and to thrive. This common factor of "being-ness," found in all that exists, is what Scotus called *the univocity of being* (*univocus*: *uni* = one + *voc* or *vox* = voice). Because of the univocity of being we can speak about God, recognize God's activity in ordinary life experiences and communicate our understandings of the world to others. Because of the univocity of being, scientific and other methods of study and learning about our world can be created and utilized.

COGNITIVE THEORY

Human Ways of Knowing: Two Kinds of Knowledge

For our purposes it is important to understand how Scotus applied his cognitive theory (understanding of intellectual knowledge) to the human capacity to know and be known by God. Scotus's cognitive theory emerges from the theological context. The Subtle Doctor studied the kind of knowledge Christ experienced while on this earth, and by extension, drew conclusions concerning the cognitive capacity of humans. Scotus optimistically concluded that all humans could participate in all of the human perfections of Jesus.

In Scotus's system, metaphysical reflection is attention given to the conceptual framework that grounds concrete experience by focusing on *abstraction*. In the act of abstraction, information is first gathered from our senses; then, it is interpreted by the imagination that presents us with a mental image; that image, in turn, gives birth to a concept or idea. Similarly, the mind can make a formal distinction, that is, it can consider something from two or more perspectives. For example, I see Paul standing in the hallway. I can recognize that he is both my brother and a mathematics teacher. All the while, I have only Paul in view.

In Scotus's system, theology deals with the contingent experiences of God revealed in Scripture[105] by focusing on *intuition* and the contingent order. Intuition is the mental activity in which the mind is immediately aware of the object it perceives; there is no mental image presented to the imagination for interpretation, as is the case in the act of abstraction. Intuition is possible because of the presence of the object "in all its proper intelligibility" and not via a mental representation or image.[106] Intuitive cognition is judged superior to abstractive cognition, because it is immediate knowledge and does not depend on a mental species or phantasm (a mental picture or image).[107] Intuitive cognition grasps the object solely in itself and in the act of experience.[108]

On the one hand, intuitive cognition can occur only with an existing object.[109] On the other hand, abstractive cognition can occur with an existing as well as a non-existing object. Abstractive knowledge is proper to scientific reflection as understood by Aristotle.

Intuitive intellection is imperfect. However in the beatific vision, both abstractive and intuitive knowledge will be perfected. (See more below.)[110]

Human Knowing and God Revealing

Scotus claimed that an object that one observes face to face and which communicates itself to the person through its actual existence and presence causes intuitive knowledge.[111] Therefore, the actual understanding gained through this kind of intellectual knowledge is necessarily a real and actual relation, connecting it to the object itself.[112]

Referring to Augustine's *De Trinitate IX*, Scotus indicates that human knowledge of God is contingent upon the divine will. When a human person knows God, movements of the will of *both* God and the person are involved. A mutual relation is thus established between the knower (human) and the known (God).[113] Human knowledge of God is not necessary knowing, as is the case with our knowledge of natural objects. However, Scotus holds that when the human mind encounters God's self-communication and apprehends it, it cannot withhold its assent to the truth of God's reality.[114] In short, God's love and God's truth are so pure and enticing that we simply fall in love and melt into God's embrace.

Personal Divine Relationship

Now, God does not communicate with humans in just any way or at any time at random. Rather, because God's nature and mode of being are personal, says Scotus, God communicates in a personal manner. Here Scotus (in contrast to Aquinas, who follows Boethius's idea of person) aligns himself with Richard of St. Victor and derives his understanding of person from reflection on the economic Trinity.[115] For Scotus, "person" is properly understood as both a relational and an ontological concept.[116] The relationship is not simply a product of our understanding. Since human logic and abstractive knowledge cannot achieve that understanding, thus prohibiting us from knowing God in God's own personal mode of being, God must be spoken of in terms of imperfect intuitive knowledge.

Scotus calls human knowledge of God a *scientia practica* because it functions through various ways and levels of knowing, each level tending toward the ultimate end (the beatific vision, experiencing the divine presence)–knowing God.[117] The process of knowing God remains real, actual and personal, however, because God freely chooses to manifest Self to us, and we, upon apprehending God as proper object, will to yield our minds to Truth and God-likeness.[118]

Revelation of the Human as Imago Dei

In addition, God reveals Self to us in Holy Scripture.[119] The Scriptures reveal that humans were created in God's own image and likeness (Gen. 1:26). Even though humans may come to realize that their source is God, they cannot naturally and fully grasp the image of God within their souls. The limitations of human cognition allow humans to know only one aspect of the God-human relationship, i.e., from the human side. In addition to what philosophy can tell us about humanity, revelation (such as Genesis 1 and 2) is needed in order for us to grasp some notion of how we are related to God.[120] Scotus relies on revelation to further explicate the relationship between God and humans in his discussion of the divine action *ad extra*, specifically the Incarnation and *acceptatio*.

Perfection of Human Knowledge of God

Humans are created with an innate desire to know and relate to the Divine.[121] God can reveal Self to the created intellect as an immediate object of vision. In the beatific vision (experiencing the divine presence), the most complete exercise of human cognition takes place. The beatific vision is not an added level of knowledge, but rather it is a gift of the free choice of the divine will for divine self-revelation. The curtain is pulled back and what has been hidden is now made manifest.

The fullness of human cognitive powers will not be realized until we experience the beatific vision.[122] Human knowledge of God is then worked out in mutual relationship between God and humans. In the beatific vision, the human intellect will enjoy the fullness of its cognitive power in a single act that unifies both intuitive and abstractive powers. At that moment direct knowledge of the divine essence will provide both immediate awareness of the presence and existence of God (intuitive cognition) precisely as God (abstractive cognition).

Self-awareness and awareness of the other are united. The process of humans coming to know God is mutual because it is a real, actual and personal exchange between divine and human. It is rooted in the relationship of the mind to reality as created by God–a relationship that manifests itself in the univocal concept of "being" and how this concept mediates the journey of our natural reflection from the world to God. The journey itself takes a lifetime to complete. What is confused and indistinct in the present life will be perfected in eternity, when we experience God as infinite, loving, gracious being.

THE INCARNATION

Intended before All Time

Without a doubt, the most profound and perfect self-revelation of God took place in the Incarnation. God, the divine artist conceived of the best way in which the fullness of divine glory could be shared. Like a diligent artist who envisions a gorgeous landscape and who then begins to execute the design by creating the background that will support the whole of the work, so too, before the beginning of time, Scotus contends, God freely planned the Incarnation.[123] Simply stated, according to Scotus, the reason for the Incarnation, in the first place, was God's free and eternal decision to have, outside God's own self, someone who could love God perfectly. Through the humanity of Jesus, God expressed the absolutely free divine desire to communicate divine love in a contingent and finite world.

And so it was that the world was created through the Word (Jn. 1:1-18). Humans were created having the capacity to respond freely to divine initiative and capable of entering into a personal relationship with God and with one another. As Scotus sees it, humans were not only created in the image and likeness of God (*imago Dei*), they were also created in the image of the incarnate Son (*imago Christi*). Just as Bonaventure taught, Scotus also sees Christ as the pattern after which all creation is fashioned. Like the Seraphic Doctor, the Subtle Doctor holds that progress in the spiritual life is a process of *christification* as well as *deification*; the more Christ-like one becomes, the more God-like one is. Indeed, human union with God is mediated through the Incarnation.

Scotus joins a long line of Franciscan scholars in maintaining that the Word would have become incarnate even if Adam had not sinned.[124] Adam's sin was not the *sine qua non* (the absolute and only cause) for the Incarnation. In Scotus's view, the Incarnation was not necessitated by the human choice to sin, for that would have effectively subjected God (who is absolutely free) to the permission of sin. Also, if the Incarnation had been the result of sin, humans would have reason, contrary to charity, to rejoice at the sinfulness of others.[125]

Rather, the Incarnation represents the manifestation of God's eternal glory and God's intent to raise human nature to the highest point of glory by uniting it with the divine nature. Understood in this way, the Incarnation is a paradigm for divine-human mutuality.

> Mutuality between God and humanity was foreseen from eternity, begun in the Incarnation and is to be fully realized in the future when Christ will be "all in all." The summit of creation is the communion of all persons with one another and with God. . . .Christ is the very person in whom the human and divine achieve mutuality.[126]

Christ embodies the divine message that human actions are pleasing to God, human persons are pleasing to God and humans are loved by God. The fact that, according to Scotus, God's freedom and liberality inspired the Incarnation provides a positive enhancement of human nature that is not possible in a sin-centric understanding of the doctrine. God, in Scotus's view, is a creative artist who selected human nature as the "material" most fitting to receive the highest glory of subsisting in the person of the Word.[127] This divine message provides the basis for Scotus's understanding of divine *acceptatio* and the order of merit. (See more below.)

Relationships Made Possible: Human and Divine

As Scotus sees it, both in creation and through salvation history, God sets out a design for human life to be lived in relationship with the Divine and with others. In fact Scotus's principle of *essential order* gives an explanation of this design, using the language of metaphysics. Another way to talk about this relational design is to use the language of *natural law*. Reasoning human beings can observe a kind of order in the created world without any kind of special divine revelation. They can see cycles in nature, or they might observe that human beings who are treated in a disrespectful manner have lower self-esteem, perhaps even leading to psychotic breakdowns.

However, Scotus explains that the Scriptures (revelation) fine-tune what we can know about relationships with God and other creatures from the natural law and place it in the context of God's love for humanity. Thus, there is a qualitative difference in how we live. In light of God's love for us, we need to consider not only whether an action is reasonable (rational judgment) but also whether the act is motivated by love (affective motivation). For example: At Christmastime, person "A" may donate to the Boys and Girls' Club because she genuinely cares about the quality of life children have, especially poor children. This is a reasonably good thing to do. In another instance, person "B," another caring person, also wants to make life better for poor children. However, she knows some of the children, because she meets them on her way to work every day. She has grown attached to them and, though she cannot afford to give each child what she or he might need, she knows they all participate in the Boys and Girls' Club. Thus, she can help all of them by giving to the club. In either scenario, a good deed is done. However, the deed in the second scenario is qualitatively (subjectively) distinct from the first, because "B" has a relationship with the children.

When Scotus discusses the summary of God's covenant with the people of Israel given in the Ten Commandments, he explains that the first table (Commandments 1-3) deals with our relationship with God (necessary realities), while the second table (Commandments 4-10) deals with relationships between neighbors (contingent realities). He claims that the meaning of the first three commandments is obvious to anyone who recognizes that God is the highest, most perfect being, namely that God is to be loved, unconditionally (*Deus diligendus est*). Significantly, we can know the commandments of the second table through the natural law. Yet, if we understand them in light of the first table, we can see that the reason we are to act lovingly toward our neighbors is not because we are great humanitarians, but rather because God deeply loves us and desires that we love one another. In this light, the Ten Commandments are no longer chapters of a legal code, but themes of a love song about our relationship to God, neighbors and all creatures.

THE HUMAN PERSON AS ETHICAL BEING

Human Free Will and Affections

A central notion of John Duns Scotus's ethical thought is that the human person is created by God and endowed with free will. According to Scotus, our human will has two affections or orientations. The first, *affectio commodi*, is directed inward toward a healthy kind of self-preservation or happiness. This is not to be understood as "selfishness." Rather, it is self-interest, a mature self-esteem that enables and requires persons to grow in integrity and to place themselves in perspective with others, while not permitting others to disrespect or abuse them.[128] The second, *affectio iustitiae*, is directed outward toward others. It seeks what is just and desires to love each individual according to his or her worth (what is rightly due them). Right living requires that we balance these two affections when making choices about things that we do or things that will shape our character. If we follow our affection for justice, Ingham states, "The result is a dynamic of mutual love and expanding inclusivity."[129] Such a stance would also enable us to live into the right relationships characteristic of the Reign of God. This, according to Ingham, would require each of us to develop *a self-reflexive stance* toward our own lives, *a critical awareness of injustice* around us and the *courage to act as quickly as possible* on behalf of justice.[130]

Human Will and Freedom of Choice

In Scotus's ethical thought, the focus is on the person; the object of moral science is the perfection of the moral person.[131] For Scotus, the will is the sole rational faculty capable of self-determination and self-movement. The *will* is a term for the human person's capacity to desire, love and choose.[132] It can will, nil, or refrain from passing judgment on any object.[133] The *intellect* is the term for the human cognitive capacity to know and to understand. While these faculties are formally distinct, they work together in the human process of choosing. Like a host who introduces a speaker to an audience, the intellect presents an idea or an object (that it has attained through either abstract or intuitive knowledge) to the will. The will then considers the possibilities and makes a choice. The significant point here is that the will *also* has access to the intellect in the process of choice making. Thus, we can place any one particular choice in perspective with other factors and choose intelligently and wisely. Scotus was clear that nothing outside of the will determines its choice. This means that even though humans can be forced to act against their will, each person is responsible for the choices he or she makes. Human freedom then is set in the context of moral rationality in the form of self-control and self-determination according to the light of reflection.[134]

The morally good act and its circumstances are determined by right reason or prudence and must be suitable to the agent, have a suitable object and be performed under suitable circumstances (end, manner, time and place).[135] Love for God is, for Scotus, the self-evident first principle of praxis. He demonstrates in *De Primo Principio* that God is infinite being and therefore also infinite goodness.[136] Then he restates the Aristotelian/Stoic maxim, "Good is to be pursued, evil avoided," as the theological principle, *Deus diligendus est.* That God is to be loved is necessarily true, because God is infinite goodness and as such, worthy of all love.

TRINITY:
BASIS FOR REALITY AND RELATIONSHIPS

Scotus's entire understanding of reality is informed by his relational apprehension of the doctrine of the Trinity. Particularly rich is the distinction he makes between the activity of the Trinity *ad intra* and *ad extra*. The life of the Trinity *ad intra* is the internal aspect of Trinitarian life in which God functions necessarily only in relation to the other persons of the Trinity. The life of the Trinity *ad extra* is that aspect whereby the Trinity expresses its divine will, freely choosing creation, Incarnation and *acceptatio*.[137] Scotus asserts that the essence of God involves both aspects of Trinitarian life, however. Of the two dimensions, the incommunicable (internal) dimension is seen as the logical *suppositum*,[138] which is necessary for the *ad extra* relationship.

In Scotus's view, the basis for the relationship among the three persons reveals an important aspect of God's essence. In his lectures discussing the constitution of the divine persons, Scotus argues for some kind of constitutive cause for each person of the Trinity.[139] Scotus finds that each of the persons and the relationship or communion of the three persons are essential to the divine life.[140] By insisting on the integrity of each person of the Trinity in the absolute sense, he designates the basis upon which he can later assert that God's essence is also communion. There can be no relationship without at least two terms joined in interaction.[141] Scotus is most clear about how God's essence is also communion in his discussion of the topic in the fourth of the *Quodlibetal Questions*.[142]

Scotus's discussion of the Trinity is significant for understanding mutuality as fundamental to human relationship for two reasons:

- Scotus's affirmation of the individual personhood of each member of the Trinity as a *suppositum* of divine relations makes it possible for the Trinity to stand as a paradigm for human relations.

- The individuality Scotus claims for each person of the Trinity provides the metaphysical basis for mutuality; the persons of the Trinity are constituted *as persons* through the relationship (*ad intra*) of mutuality. Insofar as the Trinity as a communion of persons models the goal for human community, the Trinity models the relationship of mutuality as the goal of all human activity.[143]

DIVINE *ACCEPTATIO*
AND THE ORDER OF MERIT

At the summit of creation is the human person, created by and for love. The *acceptatio* of the divine is God's acceptance of any morally good human action inspired by charity (love) and the establishment of a reward for those actions. In the order of merit, the human moral act is informed by charity and the reward intended by God is established by the divine will. In the process of God's acceptance, the human moral act is judged worthy of divine acceptance, enhanced by divine liberality and generosity and then rewarded beyond the action's natural value.[144]

In contrast to the naturally good act (an act that only complies with natural law), the moral act must be chosen freely in accord with right reason, deal with an appropriate object and be influenced by the virtues of faith, hope and love.[145] Scotus attempted to determine the precise capacity of humans for good.[146] He concluded that the human capacity for goodness, based on love, extends automatically to acts of charity or generosity out of love for God.

Scotus sets up a dialogical model for human/divine relationship in the prayer at the beginning of his *Tractatus de primo principio*, citing the Covenant with Moses in Exodus 3:15.[147] Scotus defines merit as a relationship to divine acceptance that confers reward upon the human act. The order of merit is the fullness of mutuality between the divine and human wills.[148] As Ingham explains:

> God in no way merits for the person, nor does divine acceptance provide the entire basis; the act must be inspired by charity and performed by right reasoning. The meritorious act is truly mine. . . ."[T]he act of merit is in my power, supposing general influence, if I have use of free will and grace." The divine act completes the human by ordaining it to the end to which natural reason aspires but is incapable of attaining: full union with God. . . ."[B]ut completion of the essence of merit is only in my dispositive power, finally to be so disposed that from divine disposition there follows the completion of my action."[149]

The unknown element in the order of merit is how much beyond its value God will reward a meritorious act (divine liberality).[150] Divine liberality is a cause for optimism and hope for the future of humanity. It is a free relationship that exists within reality for both the human and the divine and that constitutes the dignity of the person and the value of each human act. In charity and freedom, humans choose the "good," and God rewards their efforts out of divine liberality and *acceptatio*.

Divine revelation characterizes Jesus Christ as "the image of the invisible God" (Col. 1:15-18), who unites all creatures with God and one another. In Ephesians 1:3-10, St. Paul speaks of "God's hidden plan," the intent of which was, from the beginning, to bring everything together under Christ. Here then, we see the divine intention is to bring all of creation to grace and glory along two distinct but unifying paths (1) the Incarnation and (2) divine *acceptatio*, in which, through grace, humans are rewarded beyond the demands of justice.[151] Both paths also serve as ground for mutuality between God and humankind.

Scotus's optimistic view of humankind ultimately flows from his refusal to identify human sin as the sole reason for the Incarnation. As we have seen, Scotus's cognitive theory outlines how humans become privy to insights concerning God's nature and actions in history. In the relationship that is willed by both God and humans, there is fluidity and continuity of divine initiative and human response in love and a redemptive advance in history toward the glory of the Beatific Vision. Scotus's moral theory demonstrates how the human will is constituted to respond not only to God's initiative but to all good it encounters (*affectiones commodi* and *affectiones justitiae*). Human efforts toward doing good are perfected in the order of merit through God's *acceptatio* and the reward of human actions inspired by charity.

Thus, we have, in Scotus, the grounding for mutuality as the primary foundational and normative manner for human relationships—with God, with other humans and with the cosmos. Indeed, mutuality names the human/divine partnership in ongoing creation and redemption.

SUMMARY:
LESSONS FROM BL. JOHN DUNS SCOTUS

1. God, who is absolutely free and perfectly loving, chose to create human beings in the divine image and likeness and sustain them in mutual relationship. This is a great affirmation of the value of humanity.

2. The Incarnation was not dependent on human sin. On the contrary, God intended the Incarnation from the beginning of time.

God confirmed the value of human life by choosing human flesh as the medium most fitting to join with the divine in the Incarnation.

3. Inviolable dignity is not given to humans *only* in a general way, as a species. Scotus's principle of *haecceitas* holds that *each distinct individual person* has a particular dignity that must be reverenced and honored. Indeed, each creature of the created world bears this distinctiveness and must be respected accordingly.

4. Humans are intelligent and free beings created by God, who is absolutely free and absolutely loving. The human response to God is to live in a manner that is intelligently and responsibly free and deeply loving. There is no moral legalism here. Obedience to God comes from love, not fear of punishment.

5. Scotus shows how the life of the Trinity provides a model for unity and mutual love. The Subtle Doctor holds Trinitarian life in mutual relationship as a foundational model for relationships between God, creatures, humans with one another, and between the divine and human as co-creators and redeemers of the world.

6. We need to pay attention to the two affections of the human will—the affection for happiness and the affection for justice. When these are in harmony and balanced in us, we are healthy persons of integrity and we can be genuinely caring and loving. If we find ourselves living exclusively out of one affection or the other, there is cause for concern, because therein, says Scotus is the occasion for sin.

7. The deep desire of God is that humans return to final communion with the divine in the Beatific Vision. In marvelous acts of love, God accepts all human efforts to love (*acceptatio*), bringing our efforts to completion and perfection, fulfilling the divine intention and the order of love. Our honest and integral efforts to live in love and in God's presence are found worthy, profoundly respected and generously affirmed and supported by God. Herein lies great hope for humanity!

QUESTIONS FOR DISCUSSION

1. How do you exercise your personal power and authority? Would Francis approve? Would Clare approve?

2. Most Catholics have never heard the Franciscan approach to the reason for the Incarnation–namely, that God planned it from before all time. Does this matter? How might you share this good news with your family? friends? parish?

3. Place your hand side by side with the hand of another person. In silence, spend five minutes comparing what you see. Is *haecceitas* a reality yet today? What difference does *haecceitas* make in your daily life? Explain.

4. Are your affection for happiness and affection for justice in harmony these days? What helps you keep the right balance?

5. In your experience, is the Decalogue more like a legal code or a love song?

PART FIVE
CONCLUSION

Some theologies of the past focused primarily on the grandeur of God's holiness. Franciscan theology certainly does not miss the holiness of God. But, beginning with Francis, who could never forget the remarkable humility of God in taking on human form in Jesus, Franciscan theologians focus on how God is present in and through the human person and in our routine, mundane and ordinary lives (incarnational theology). Francis, Clare, Bonaventure, Scotus–each in his or her own way–tell the story of the human only in relationship with God. Succeeding theologians begin their discussion of the human with God in Christ, set us on the path to follow Jesus and end the discussion with our return to God through the saving work of Christ. As we have seen, three themes–dignity, mediation and mutuality–summarize central elements of this Franciscan theology of the human person. In all of the discussion, we find that humans are created in the very image and likeness of God, are relational beings, are embodied subjects, are historical subjects, and are fundamentally equal, though uniquely original.

Image and Likeness of God

Beginning with the accounts of Genesis, special attention is given to the creation of the human person and to the relationship of the human with God. While God placed humans among the other creatures, God created humans separately from the other animals (Gen. 1:26-27). In a unique act of creation, God also shared with humans the very divine breath of life (Gen. 2:7). Thus began the long and deep Jewish and Christian tradition that holds that humans bear *the divine image and likeness* and stand in special relationship to other creatures, to one another and to God. Saying that humans bear the "image of God" says something about God and something about humanity.

63

Something about God

As the creation narratives imply, there is a special relationship between humans and God. God's most definitive characteristic is that
"God is love" (1 Jn. 4:8, 16). It is God's love and care that overflow,
bringing about creation–especially humans–and sustains it. Humanity is thus related to God in such a thoroughgoing way that being in
the "image of God" is an irreversible condition. It is the case that
humans cannot be properly understood without a relationship to
God. Just as God relates lovingly and justly to all creation, so too
humans must engage in loving and just relationships.

Something about Humans

Bearing the "image of God" also speaks volumes about humanity.
God, who is a communion of three persons (Trinity), created humans to be social beings. The social and universal implications of
bearing God's image include the fact that people share a common
condition and a common end in God. The more we participate in
life in community with our sisters and brothers, the more we come
to know our true selves. If we fail to share life deeply with others,
withholding our gifts and refusing to receive the talents and insights
from others, the humanity of all is diminished. Jesus, in the
"Franciscan Gospel" of John, put it this way: "As I have loved you,
so you must love one another" (Jn. 13:34). To be fully human, we
must live as God lives and love as God loves.

Relational Beings

In order to love one another truly and concretely in our pluralistic,
ecologically threatened world, we need to recall those basic ways in
which all humans might be reverenced and respected.[152] First, we
must realize that all humans are created as *relational beings*, fundamentally interdependent with one another in all dimensions of life.
Humans are at their best when living in healthy relationship with
God, self, other people and all of creation. Thus, all political, economic, or social structures, if they are to be just, must form and

promote the kind of interdependence modeled for us by the trinitarian life of God.

Embodied Subjects

Secondly, each human person is also an *embodied subject*; that is, each person has the capacity for self-determination and freedom; each has a distinct conscience. We cannot escape our physical bodies–nor should we try–because they are "very good"(Gen. 1:27-28, 31; 2:25) and a source of our personal uniqueness. As part of the material world, we are somewhat limited by our physical bodies, yet we have great potential as co-creators with God and the capacity to use our bodies to make the world a more lovable and livable place.

Historical Subjects

Thirdly, we are *historical subjects*. Though we are embodied, material beings, we are also spiritual beings, the material world made conscious.[153] We move through daily life, writing our own story as we journey on our way to God. From the moment of our conception, each of us grows and changes, potentially developing and emerging into a more fully conscious, better-integrated, loving human person. Each act, thought or feeling has consequences toward molding us and forming the world and the people we touch. For better or worse, we have the awesome power to love one another into life or to desecrate the God-given dignity of another.

Fundamentally Equal, though Uniquely Original

Finally, it is our God-given dignity that makes all peoples *fundamentally equal*. Yet, at the same time, each person is *uniquely original*; there are no two people alike. Two people looking at the same thing will ultimately describe what they are seeing differently because each has a distinct imagination and life experience. Yet, without too much difficulty, we can identify some "basic human needs" such as food, clothing, shelter and rest that are common to all people everywhere.

None of the Franciscans were content to simply collect knowledge about God and humanity. They were eager to bring their knowledge and reflections to bear on the ordinary lives of real people. In their time they did what was theirs to do. In the spirit of St. Francis, let us begin with what is ours to do!

QUESTIONS FOR DISCUSSION

1. Is there hope for humanity? Why?

2. In all integrity, how have you noticed yourself growing more Christ like? What helps you to keep living this way? What hinders?

APPENDIX

Tabernacles

Graziano Marcheschi

It happened fast.
A feeble-brained innocent,
    refugee from half-way spaces, moving at the wrong time:
    the Bread raised high,
    the Cup engaged in mystery,
and he chooses this time to change his seat
from one church side to the other.
For a moment his head blocks the view
of bread yielding to miracle.
For a moment his face and the bread are one.
The words spoken over both.
Then hands shake, extending proper peace;
cheeks meet,
words wish a peace the world has never tasted.
He stares, like a dog offered too many bones at once,
and accepts only one hand's greeting.
Next comes procession to his first meal of the day
as faces clearly wonder if he understands what this is all about.
He takes the proffered piece of pita
    in this most post-Vatican assembly
and stops.
Momentarily thrown by this bread with pockets,
he's oh-so-gently reassured that it's quite all right to eat.
He takes
and green teeth masticate the Body of Christ.
Then he reaches for the syrupped goodness of the cup
(Just three sips after him I debate the wisdom of changing lines.)

67

His puffed-cheek mouthful nearly drains the cup.
(I almost wish he had so I wouldn't need to tell myself I won't catch
some disease.)
And then
(I knew it!)
he coughs
and sends forth a rosy mist
that sprays Divinity onto the floor.
A rainbow comes and goes in that unexpected spray
as gasps are quelled in forty throats.
He clamps his mouth with leaky hands
looking like a child
trying to keep a pricked balloon from bursting.
Unslackened, the line moves on
and Divinity is trampled by shod feet
till pure white linen,
          –bleached and starched–
in fervent hands that won't permit impiety,
drinks the pink God from the floor.
In a corner he sits alone
in rapt humiliation.
When someone asks, "Are you O.K.?"
he quickly shows his palms and says,
"I didn't wipe them on my dirty pants, I didn't.
I rubbed them hard together, see?"
and he demonstrates, with insect frenzy, how he used friction
to evaporate the spilled God from his hands.
Oh, what a cunning God who tests our faith
by hiding in green-teethed
tabernacles
to see how truly we believe
in the miracle of real presence.[154]

REFLECTIONS ON "TABERNACLES"

Each time I read this poem, it tugs powerfully at my Franciscan heart. This "tugging" is evidence of the foundational moral experience of reverence for persons and their environment. But this reverence comes at a cost and it is often shrouded in paradox. In the Mass the cup does "engage mystery" and the bread does indeed, "yield to miracle," making the God I seek truly present. But God's presence is not *only* borne forth in the anticipated sacramental mystery. It appears simultaneously in the concrete; in the despicable "feeble brained innocent." I read on, and in a moment of recognition, recall the powerful words of the theologian, Paul Ramsey, "Call no one vile for whom Christ has died!" Yes, it is much easier to find God in the miraculous than in the ordinary! Though the Catholic faith holds that the same God is present in the bread and wine as in the flesh of the "least ones" as the *imago Dei*, I often fail to grasp the obvious!

This poem profoundly illustrates the deep link that exists, and that Franciscan theology emphasizes, between the Christian doctrines of creation and redemption; between God's generous and exquisite gift of human life itself and the even more extravagant self-gift of God in the Incarnation and in the Eucharist. The green-teethed "feeble-brained innocent" always jars me back into the reality that *the same Christ Incarnate* redeems *all people*, and, therefore, divisions of any sort are most certainly idolatrous. One can only imagine that reflections similar to these flashed through the mind and heart of Francis and Clare of Assisi as they experienced the sick and poor—especially the lepers of their day.

I often use this poem in my opening lecture for the Introduction to Christian Ethics course I teach at Catholic Theological Union in Chicago. Unprompted, my students who come from all over the globe, identify with the narrator as they wrestle with the more abstract considerations of liturgical propriety, sacrosanct piety and with the more concrete concerns of personal health, the material nauseating mess of regurgitated wine, feelings of genuine concern for the man and the nagging in-breaking of God's revelation in every moment. Listening to this story, my students find themselves being led from what *is* actually going on to what *should* be taking place. The narrator, in this "most post-Vatican assembly," presumably *should* be aware of the inviolable dignity of the person and the Council's mandate to serve the real material needs of the poor.[155] Yet, only at the end does the narrator finally awaken to the miracle of God's self-revelation in the "green-teethed tabernacle." The students often state that this scene taps into their "gut feeling that there is something more going on here than stupidity, impropriety or sacrilege."

The very meaning of the Eucharist in Catholic worship proclaims the deep unity of the created and the redeemed, of the divine and the human. It speaks of including all at the table. It reveals the *image of God* in humanity, made holy because of God's choice to take on human flesh in the person of the poor Christ. Yet, in our day, there are so many times when we look for Christ in the "high places" of orderliness, self-sufficiency, sanitary conditions, or proper associations. In such activities, we miss finding Christ in the "green-teethed tabernacles" of our day such as our own sisters or brothers, persons with AIDS, the elderly poor, refugees, or illegal aliens.

Like Francis and Clare who were converted to the poor and the lepers, the narrator of this poem finally got the message. God profoundly reveals Godself in the ordinary events of human life, but perhaps most significantly in human relationships. Do you and I "get the message"? How does that affect the way we live?

ENDNOTES

[1]Daniel C. Maguire, *The Moral Choice* (Garden City: Doubleday and Company, Inc., 1978), 172.

[2]Karl Rahner, S.J. "Anthropology," in Karl Rahner and Herbert Vorgrimler, eds., *Theological Dictionary* (New York: Herder & Herder, 1965), 25-28.

[3]See Appendix, p. 67, for the poem, "Tabernacles," Graziano Marcheschi, *Wheat and Weeds and the Wolf of Gubbio: Stories and Prayers for People Who Pray and for People Who Don't* (Kansas City, MO: Sheed and Ward, 1994), 5-7.

[4]For more details on this see Duane V. Lapsanski, *Evangelical Perfection: An Historical Examination of the Concept in the Early Franciscan Sources* (St. Bonaventure, NY: The Franciscan Institute, 1977). Also see Marilyn Hammond, "St. Francis as Struggling Hermeneut," in Jay M. Hammond, ed., *Francis of Assisi: Historiography, Hagiography and Hermeneutics in the Early Documents* (Hyde Park, NY: New City Press, 2004), especially 220-24. See Ingrid J. Peterson, O.S.F., *Clare of Assisi: A Biographical Study* (Quincy, IL: Franciscan Press, 1993), 212-13 and 322-24.

[5]See *The Legend of Clare* 1:1, in Regis J. Armstrong, O.F.M. Cap., *Clare of Assisi: Early Documents*, revised and expanded (St. Bonaventure, NY: The Franciscan Institute, 1993), 252-3. (All references to the writings of Clare and her early biographical sources are from this work unless otherwise noted; henceforth indicated as CA:ED.)

[6]See Duane V. Lapsanski, *The First Franciscans and the Gospel* (Chicago: Franciscan Herald Press, 1976), especially 15-61.

[7]John of St. Paul had been the papal legate to an Albigensian territory, 1200-1201. See Herbert Gründmann, *Religiose Bewegüngen in Mittelalter* (Darmstadt: Wissenschaftliche Buchgesellschaft, 1961), 130.

[8]See the *Earlier Rule*, Chapter 23, and the *Letter to the Faithful* for examples.

[9]See Carolyn Walker Bynum, *Fragmentation and Redemption: Essays on Gender and the Human Body in Medieval Religion* (New York: Zone Books, 1991), 11.

[10]Numerous examples of Francis's experience and teaching concerning the body and asceticism can be found throughout the Franciscan sources. Some of the most interesting for our purposes are:

<u>Positive</u>: Francis ate grapes with a sick brother–see "Assisi Compilation," 53, in *Francis of Assisi: Early Documents*, Vol. II, ed. Regis J. Armstrong, O.F.M.Cap., J. A. Wayne Hellmann, O.F.M. Conv., William J. Short, O.F.M. (New York: New City Press, 2000), 152. (Henceforth FA:ED plus volume number); Francis held a conversation about his own treatment of his body and at the end of the conversation he apologized to "Brother Body": see Thomas of Celano, "The Remembrance of the Desire of a Soul," 210-11, FA:ED, II, 382-38; Francis permitted sick friars to wear soft clothing under their rough habit: see "A Mirror of Perfection," Sabatier Edition, 1:15, FA:ED, III, 267; Francis warned against excessive abstinence from food: see "A Mirror of Perfection" Sabatier Edition, 27, FA:ED, III, 278-79; Francis gave advice to meet the needs of Brother Body: see "A Mirror of Perfection," Sabatier Edition, 97, FA:ED, III, 344.

<u>Negative</u>: Francis was always concerned that his laxity in bodily discipline would not only harm him spiritually, but it would be a poor example for the friars: see "Assisi Compilation," 82, in FA:ED, II, 184; see also "A Mirror of Perfection,"

Sabatier Edition, 16, FA:ED, III, 268 and "A Mirror of Perfection," Lemmens Edition, 39, FA:ED, IIII, 247; Francis, sick and in pouring rain, got off his horse and walked while he prayed the Hours: see "Assisi Compilation," 120, FA:ED, II, 229; bodily existence was a kind of separation from God, so constant prayer was necessary to remain in God's presence: see Bonaventure, "The Major Legend of St. Francis," 10:1, FA:ED, II, 605; Francis gave a brother the penance to strip naked and ask a poor man he had insulted for forgiveness: see "A Mirror of Perfection," Lemmens Edition, 42, FA:ED, III, 249-50; when Francis ate special food during Lent, he had the brothers lead him naked and with a rope around his neck through the city: see "A Mirror of Perfection," Sabatier Edition, 61, 63, FA:ED, III, 305-07. See also, Marilyn Hammond, "St. Francis as Struggling Hermeneut," 220-24. For sources on Clare, see *Clare of Assisi: Early Documents*, 24.

[11]All references to Francis's writings and early biographies are from FA:ED.

[12]See also Thomas Aquinas, *Summa Theologia*, I-II, 112.1 and II-II, 25.1, 6, 8, 12.

[13]See also Adm 1:8-9.

[14]Verses 1-9 were composed first. Then verses 10-11 were composed to confront he quarreling between a civil and a religious authority. Verses 12-13 were written on Francis's deathbed.

[15]Some scholars have argued that Francis was a kinesthetic learner–he needed to have "hands on" experience to really understand something. So the experience of the bodily wounds of Jesus was instructive for his conversion in many ways. See Marilyn Hammond, n. 55 in "St. Francis as Struggling Hermeneut," 223.

[16]Thomas Murtaugh, "St. Francis and Ecology," in Dawn M. Nothwehr, O.S.F., ed., *Franciscan Theology of the Environment: An Introductory Reader* (Quincy, IL: Franciscan Press, 2002), 107.

[17]Eric Doyle, O.F.M., "The Canticle of Brother Sun and the Value of Creation," in Nothwehr, ed., *Franciscan Theology of the Environment: An Introductory Reader*, 155-74.

[18]Doyle, 158.

[19]Doyle, 161.

[20]Doyle, 164.

[21]Leonardo Boff, *Cry of the Earth, Cry of the Poor*, trans. Phillip Berryman (Maryknoll: Orbis Books, 1997), 187-202.

[22]"He continued with great intensity of spirit: 'allow me to rejoice in the Lord, Brother, and to sing His praises in my infirmities, because, by the grace of the Holy Spirit, I am so closely united and joined with my Lord that, through His mercy, I can well rejoice in the Most High Himself.'"

[23]For a discussion of possible reasons for this, see Margaret Carney, "Franciscan Women and the Theological Enterprise," in Kenan B. Osborne, O.F.M., ed., *The History of Franciscan Theology* (St. Bonaventure, NY: The Franciscan Institute, 1994), 331-45, especially at 333.

[24]*Process of Canonization*, 1:1-2, CA:ED, 136.

[25]See *The Legend of Clare*, 5, CA:ED, 256-57.

[26]See the "Privilege of Poverty of Innocent III (1216)," CA:ED, 85-86 and "The Form of Life of Pope Innocent IV (1247)," CA:ED, 113-28.

[27]CA:ED, 30.

[28]CA:ED, 59.

[29]CA:ED, 50-51.

[30]CA:ED, 51.

[31]CA:ED, 42. See also *Fourth Letter to Agnes*, 15-23, CA:ED, 50-1.

[32]See *Process of Canonization*, 1:1 and 2:12, in CA:ED, 139 and144; or *The Legend of St. Clare*, 28, CA:ED, 282.

[33]*Process of Canonization*, 9:2, CA:ED, 165.

[34]This is the most consistently reported event in the life of Clare. See Armstrong, *Process of Canonization*, n. *a*, CA:ED, 146.

[35]*Form of Life of Clare*, 2:3-4, CA:ED, 65.

[36]*Form of Life of Clare*, 15, CA:ED, 68.

[37]*Form of Life of Clare*, 14, CA:ED, 68.

[38]CA:ED, 40.

[39]See, for example, these words of Clare: *First Letter to Agnes*, 17, CA:ED, 36; *Second Letter to Agnes*, 2, CA:ED, 40; *Second Letter to Agnes*, 18-20 CA:ED, 42; *Testament of Clare*, 56, CA:ED, 56; and *Form of Life of Clare*, 2, CA:ED, 63.

[40]CA:ED, 63.

[41]See the *Process of Canonization* for these and numerous other healings attributed to Clare.

[42]CA:ED, 45.

[43]Elizabeth A. Dreyer, "'[God] Whose Beauty the Sun and the Moon Admire,' Clare and Ecology," in Nothwehr, ed., *Franciscan Theology of the Environment: An Introductory Reader*, 129-41.

[44]Dreyer, 133-34.

[45]Margaret Carney, O.S.F., *The First Franciscan Woman: Clare of Assisi and Her Form of Life* (Quincy, IL: Franciscan Press, 1993), 159.

[46]*Form of Life of Clare*, 9:6-10, CA:ED, 75-6.

[47]*Form of Life of Clare*, 4:1-5, CA:ED, 68-9.

[48]CA:ED, 69-70.

[49]*Form of Life of Clare*, 2:15-18, 21-23; 3:1-4; 7:3-5, CA:ED, 62 n. a, 66, 67, 73.

[50]See Peterson, *Clare of Assisi*, especially Chapter 30, "Popes," for an account of how some tried to dissuade Clare from her understanding of poverty.

[51]Peterson, 219.

[52]Peterson, 282.

[53]CA:ED, 50.

[54]*Form of Life of Clare*, 3:10-11, CA:ED, 68.

[55]See Joseph Chinnici, "Francis and Clare: Praxis of Solidarity in the Contemporary World," *The Way Supplement* (1994): 17-24.

[56]Carney, *The First Franciscan Woman*, 21-63.

[57]Dreyer, "'[God] Whose Beauty'," 133.

[58]CA:ED, 52.

[59]*Process of Canonization*, 3:32, CA:ED, 153.

[60]CA:ED, 151.

[61]Boff, *Cry of the Earth, Cry of the Poor*, 31-34.

[62]Zachary Hayes, O.F.M., "Bonaventure: Mystery of the Triune God," in Osborne, ed., *The History of Franciscan Theology*, 45. See also Regis J. Armstrong, O.F.M. Cap., "Francis of Assisi and the Prisms of Theologizing" *Greyfriars Review*, 10.2 (1996): 196-98.

[63]Bonaventure, II Sent. I. 2. I. 2., fund. 3 (II. 41b) cited in Alexander Schaeffer, "The Position and Function of Man in the Created World According to Bonaventure," *Franciscan Studies* 21 (1960): 307.

[64]Zachary Hayes, O.F.M., "The Cosmos: A Symbol of the Divine," in Nothwehr, ed., *Franciscan Theology of the Environment: An Introductory Reader*, 250-51.

[65]"Metaphysics is the attempt to present a comprehensive, coherent, and consistent account (picture, view) of reality (being, universe) as a whole"; s. v. "metaphysics," in Peter A. Angeles, *Dictionary of Philosophy* (New York: Barnes and Noble Books, 1981).

[66]Hayes, "Bonaventure: Mystery," 53-60.

[67]Zachary Hayes, O.F.M., "Bonaventure: The Mystery of the Triune God," in Dawn M. Nothwehr, ed. *Franciscan Theology of the Environment: An Introductory Reader* (Quincy, IL: Franciscan Press, 2002), at 216: "In the strict sense of the word, only the Son and the Spirit can be sent, since only they come forth by emanation. Methodologically, it is only from the experience of the historical missions of the Son and the Spirit that Christians come to know the Father in a specifically Christian sense as the ultimate source of emanation and hence of mission. The entire doctrine of the incarnation is nothing but a discussion of the mission of the Son. The mission of the Spirit is discussed in the doctrine of the church and the doctrine of grace."

[68]In Chapter 2 of *The Soul's Journey into God*, Bonaventure shows how the senses bring us into contact with God.

[69]Ontology is "the branch of philosophy which attempts (a) to describe the nature of ultimate Being (The One, The Absolute, The Perfect Eternal Form), (b) to show that all things depend upon it for their existence, (c) to indicate how their dependency is mediated in reality, and (d) to relate human thoughts and actions to this reality on an individual and historical basis"; s.v. "ontology," in Peter A. Angeles, *Dictionary of Philosophy.*

[70]Hayes, "Bonaventure: Mystery," 56.

[71]See Bonaventure, *Breviloquium* 2.12 [5:230], cited in Zachary Hayes, O.F.M., *Bonaventure: Mystical Writings*, Spiritual Legacy Series (New York: Crossroad Publishing Company, 1999), 90. Note that all citations Hayes gives in this work are his translations from *Doctoris Seraphici S. Bonaventurae opera omnia*, (Quaracchi: Collegium S. Bonaventurae, 1882-1902). The first two numerals indicate the section of the text, the bracketed numerals indicate the volume and the page in that volume.

[72]Phil Hoebing, "St. Bonaventure and Ecology," in Nothwehr, ed., *Franciscan Theology of the Environment*, 276. Note that Hoebing's use of "man" is intended to include both female and male human beings.

[73]Bonaventure, *Collations on the Six Days of Creation*, 1.13 [5:332], cited in Hayes, "Bonaventure: Mystery," 74.

[74]Zachary Hayes, O.F.M., "Of God's Fullness We Have All Received: The Teaching of St. Bonaventure on Creation," a lecture given at The National Franciscan Forum, *Franciscans Doing Theology* (Franciscan Center, Colorado Springs, CO), June 12, 1997. The videocassette of the lecture is included in Mary C. Gurley, O.S.F., "An Independent Study Program to Accompany *The History of Franciscan Theology*," ed. Kenan Osborne, O.F.M. (St. Bonaventure, NY: The Franciscan Institute, 1999).

[75]See Hayes, "Bonaventure: Mystery," 63-64.

[76]Bonaventure, *The Collations on the Six Days of Creation* 3.8 [5:344], cited in Hayes, *Mystical Writings,* 73.

[77]Zachary Hayes, O.F.M., "The Cosmos," in Nothwehr, ed., *Franciscan Theology of the Environment,* 252-3.

[78]Hayes, "The Cosmos," 258. See also Hayes, "Bonaventure: Mystery," 65.

[79]Bonaventure, *The Journey of the Soul into God,* 1.15 [5:299], cited in Hayes, *Bonaventure: Mystical Writings,* 77.

[80]Bonaventure, *Itinerarium Mentis in Deum,* 3 (V, 303ff.), cited in Hayes, "Bonaventure: Mystery," 81.

[81]Hayes, "Bonaventure: Mystery," 82.

[82]Ilia Delio, O.S.F., *Simply Bonaventure: An Introduction to his Life, Thought, and Writings* (Hyde Park, NY: New City Press, 2001), 69. She cites Bonaventure, *Brev.* 2. 10 (V, 228).

[83]Bonaventure, *Brev.* II, 10, cited in Thomas A. Shannon, "Human Dignity in the Theology of St. Bonaventure," in *Franciscan Leadership in Ministry,* ed. Anthony Carrozzo, O.F.M., Vincent Cushing, O.F.M. and Kenneth Himes, O.F.M., *Spirit and Life* 7 (St. Bonaventure, NY: The Franciscan Institute, 1997): 67.

[84]Alvin Black, "The Doctrine of the Image and Similitude in Saint Bonaventure," *The Cord* 12 (1962): 270.

[85]Bonaventure, III Sent. d. 1, a. q. 3, resp. (III, 29), cited in Delio, *Simply Bonaventure,* 72.

[86]Delio, *Simply Bonaventure,* 72.

[87]Bonaventure, *Collationes in Hexaëmeron,* 12.9 (V, 386); trans. De Vinck, *Six Days of Creation,* 177, cited in Delio, *Simply Bonaventure,* 72.

[88]Alexander Schaeffer, "The Position and Function of Man in the Created World According to Bonaventure," *Franciscan Studies* 21 (1961): 320.

[89]Ewert Cousins, *Christ of the 21st Century* (Rockport, MA: Element, Inc., 1992), 152-5.

[90]See II *Sent.* prooem. (II, 1-6). English trans. Johnson, *Bonaventure,* 57, cited in Delio, *Simply Bonaventure,* 75.

[91]Delio, *Simply Bonaventure,* 75.

[92]Delio, *Simply Bonaventure,* 77. She cites the following: II *Sent.* d. 33, a.1, q.2 (II,75): II *Sent.* d.19, a.3, q.1, concl. (II, 470). See also Bonaventure Hinwood, O.F.M., "'Justice' According to St. Bonaventure," *The Cord* 31 (1981): 323-35.

[93]Delio, *Simply Bonaventure,* 79. She cites the following: Hayes, "Bonaventure: Mystery," 79-80; *Hex.* 1.24 (V, 333).

[94]Shannon, "Human Dignity in the Theology of St. Bonaventure," 69.

[95]Bonaventure, *Breviloquium* 7.4, cited by Shannon, 69.

[96]Mary Beth Ingham, C.S.J., *Scotus for Dunces: An Introduction to the Subtle Doctor* (St. Bonaventure, NY: Franciscan Institute Publications, 2003), 109, 125. She credits Henry Beck, O.F.M., with the term "beatific embrace."

[97]See Dawn M. Nothwehr, O.S.F., *Mutuality: A Formal Norm for Christian Social Ethics* (San Francisco: Catholic Scholars Press, 1998) for a full explanation of this term. Chapter Two treats the contribution of Scotus's thought as an antecedent to the feminist understanding. Simply defined, "mutuality" is a sharing of power–with, by and among all parties in a relationship–in a way that recognizes the whole-

ness and particular experience of each participant for the optimum flourishing of all.

[98]*Tractatus de primo principio*, I.8, Pars I, q.3.n.89 (IV, 195.16-18); trans. Mary Elizabeth Ingham, C.S.J., *Ethics and Freedom: An Historical Critical Investigation of Scotist Ethical Thought* (Lanham, MD: University Press of America, 1989), 20: " . . . a concept is univocal if it is sufficiently one so that it would be contradictory to affirm it or to deny it of the same object, or if taken as a middle term of a syllogism, two terms may be linked through it without fallacy of equivocation."

[99]Kenan Osborne, O.F.M., "Incarnation, Individuality, and Diversity," in Nothwehr, ed., *Franciscan Theology of the Environment: An Introductory Reader*, 299.

[100]John Duns Scotus, *Ordinatio* III.37; trans. Allan B. Wolter, O.F.M., *Duns Scotus on the Will and Morality* (Washington, DC: Catholic University of America Press, 1986), 269. See also John Duns Scotus, *Tractatus de primo principio*, 4:15; trans. Allan B. Wolter, O.F.M., *A Treatise on God as First Principle* (Chicago: Franciscan Herald Press, 1981), 82. Also see Scotus, *Ordinatio* I.44; trans. Wolter, *Will and Morality*, 255.

[101]*John Duns Scotus: God and Creatures, The Quodlibital Questions*, paperback edition; trans. Felix Alluntis and Allan B. Wolter, O.F.M. (Washington, DC: Catholic University of America Press, 1981), "Glossary," 511: "*haecceitas*, (from the Latin *haec*, this): The term means literally, "thisness." It designates the unique formal principle of individuation that makes the nature, which all individuals of the same species have in common, to be just this or that individual and no other. Scotus regards it as a distinct positive formality over and above the common nature of the individual (*natura communis*)."

[102]Eric Doyle, O.F.M., "Duns Scotus and Ecumenism," *De Doctrina I. Duns Scoti*, vol. III, Acta Congressus Scotistici Internationalis Oxonii et Edimburgi, ed. Camille Bérubé (Roma: Cura Commissionis Scotisticae, 1968), 460: "The uniqueness, the unrepeatable something of all things, is what gives them their intrinsic and eternal value. There is about everything, every person, an originality that gives new insight into reality, another aspect that has never been seen before. Each person enters into a new enriching relationship of knowledge and love with every new person met, with every new thing encountered."

[103]Ingham, *Scotus for Dunces*, 55.

[104]Ingham, *Scotus for Dunces*, 55.

[105]Ingham, *Ethics and Freedom*, 13-17.

[106]Scotus, *Quodlibet*, 14.n.10; trans. Alluntis/Wolter, 325.

[107]Scotus, *Tractatus de primo principio* IV.4.89; trans. Wolter, *First Principle*, 149.

[108]Sebastian Day, *Intuitive Cognition: A Key to the Significance of the Later Scholastics* (St. Bonaventure, NY: Franciscan Institute, 1947), 82. See T. F. Torrance, "Intuitive and Abstractive Knowledge: From Duns Scotus to John Calvin," in *De Doctrina Ioannis Duns Scoti*, ed. C. Bérubé, Acta Congressus Scotistici Internationalis Oxionii et Edimburgi, (Roma: Caria Commissionis Scotisticae, 1968), 291-305. Also, Richard Dumont, "Intuition: Prescript of Postscript in Scotus's Demonstration of God's Existence," in *Deus et Homo ad mentem I. Duns Scoti*, Acta Tertii Congressus Scotistici Internationalis, Vindebonae (Romae: Societas Internationalis Scotistica, 1972), 86.

[109]Scotus, *Quodlibet* 7.n.8 (Alluntis 7:22); trans. Alluntis/Wolter, 167.

[110]Scotus, *Quodlibet* 14.n.12 (Alluntis 14:43); trans. Alluntis/Wolter, 327.

[111] Scotus, *Ordinatio* II.d.3.q.9.n.6.7; III.d.14.q.3.n.7. The key phrase is *"causari in intellectu."*

[112]Scotus, *Quodlibet* q.13.n.34; trans. Alluntis/Wolter, 292.

[113]Scotus, *Ordinatio* prol. n.72; I.d.3.n.486-493; II.d.3.q.8.n.17.

[114]Scotus, *Metaphysics* IX.q.15.n.6; trans. Wolter, *Will and Morality*, 145. See also *Quodlibet* q.16.n.6; trans. Alluntis/Wolter, 375-76.

[115]Scotus, *Ordinatio* 1.d.23.n.15; *Reportatio* 1.d.23.q.un.n.7; *Quodlibet* q.3.n.17; trans. Alluntis/Wolter, 74-75. See also *Reportatio* 1.d.25.q.2.n.5.6.7.14; *Quodlibet* q.3.n.3; trans. Alluntis/Wolter, 69-79.

[116]Scotus, *Ordinatio* I.d.4.n.11-13; *Reportatio* I.d.25.q.2.n.5.14; d.26.q.5.n.5; *Quodlibet* q.3.n.4.6.9; q.13.n.11; q.19.n.20; trans. Alluntis/Wolter, 64-65, 68; 292-93; 435-36.

[117]Scotus, *Quodlibet* q.7.n.8; q.13.n.11; trans. Alluntis/Wolter, 166-67; 292-93. See also, *Reportatio* prol. q.2.n.17. In addition see, *Tractatus de primo* 4. n.36; trans. Wolter, *First Principle*, 98. See also Ordinatio prol.n.141.168.

[118]Scotus, *Ordinatio* prol. n. 314-15; n.210-12; III.d.1.q.1.n. 8.9; *Quodlibet* q.19. n.19; trans. Alluntis/Wolter, 423.

[119]Scotus, *Tractatus de primo* 1.n.1; trans. Wolter, *First Principle*, 2.

[120]Scotus, *Quodlibet* 14. nn. 23-24 (Alluntis 1:83) trans. Alluntis/Wolter, 338-39.

[121]Scotus, *Ordinatio* IV.d.23.q.1.n.10.11; d.25.q.1.n.9. I am grateful to Mary Beth Ingham for her kind assistance in helping me write this section in clear accessible language.

[122]Scotus, *Quodlibet* 14.10, 14.36; trans. Alluntis/Wolter, 324-5.

[123]Scotus's position on the Incarnation is articulated in his *Reportatio* and *Ordinatio* III.7.3. See Allan B. Wolter, "John Duns Scotus on the Primacy and Personality of Christ," in *Franciscan Christology: Selected Texts, Translations and Essays*, ed. Damian McElrath, O.F.M. (St. Bonaventure, NY: The Franciscan Institute, 1980), 147-55. See also Antonio Aranda, "La Cuestión Teológica de la Encarnatión del Verbo: Relectura de Tres Posiciones Características," *Scripta Theologica* 25 (1993): 49-94.

[124]See Robert North, "The Scotist Cosmic Christ," in *De Doctrina Ioannis Duns Scoti*, vol. III, 194-98. Positions of key Franciscans concerning the reason for the Incarnation are: Alexander of Hales (1200): it would have been suitable had there been no sin; Matthew of Aquasparta (1282): it was supposed for the perfection of the natural order; Raymond Lull (1289): its primary aim was to show forth the love of God; Roger Marston and William of Ware: it would have taken place "apart from sin"; Bonaventure: either position was orthodox, but he opted for the traditional Anselmian solution which held sin as the cause.

[125]Scotus, *Ordinatio* III, d.7, in *Four Questions on Mary*, 25, cited in Ingham, *Scotus for Dunces*, 77

[126]Mary Elizabeth Ingham, C.S.J., "Integrated Vision," in Osborne, ed., *The History of Franciscan Theology*, 222.

[127]Scotus, *Ordinatio* III.7.q.3; trans. Wolter, "On the Primacy," 151: "Now the sequence in which the creative artist evolves his plan is the very opposite of the way he puts it into execution. One can say, however, that in the order of execution, God's union with a human nature is really prior to his granting it the greatest grace and glory. We could presume, then, that it was in the reverse order that he intended

them, so that God would first intend that some nature, not the highest, should receive the highest glory, as he bestowed natural perfection. Then secondly, as it were, he willed that this nature should subsist in the Person of the Word, so that the angel might not be subject to a [mere] man."

[128]Scotus, *Ordinatio* II.d.6.q.2.n.8 (Vivès 12:353); trans. Wolter, *Will and Morality*, 463.

[129]Mary Elizabeth Ingham, C.S.J., "A Certain Affection For Justice," *The Cord* 45.3 (1995): 15.

[130]Ingham, "A Certain Affection," 15.

[131]*Ordinatio* prol.5.q.1-2.n.262 (Vatican I 177.11-12).

[132]Ingham, *Scotus for Dunces*, 94. She defines will and intellect in the context of faculty psychology.

[133]Scotus, *Quaestiones Metaphysicam IX*, q.15; trans. Wolter, *Will and Morality*, 145-7. See also *Ordinatio* IV.49.1.10.n.10 (Vivès 21:333b). Wolter views this position in light of self-determination or rational self-direction, which ideates the will from potency to act. See his essay "Native Freedom of the Will Key to the Ethics of Scotus," in Marilyn McCord Adams, ed., *The Philosophical Theology of John Duns Scotus* (Ithaca: Cornell University Press, 1990), 152.

[134]Ingham, *Scotus for Dunces*, 96.

[135]Scotus, *Quodlibet* 18.1.n.3.18.8 trans. Alluntis/Wolter, 400.

[136]Scotus, *Tractatus de primo principio*, 4:87-4:94; trans. Wolter, *First Principle*, 146-51. See also *Ordinatio* III, suppl.d.27; trans. Wolter, *Will and Morality*, 425: "As for the first, I say that to love God above all is an act conformed to natural right reason, which dictates that what is best must be loved most; and hence such an act is right in itself; indeed, as a first practical principle of action, this is something known *per se*, and hence its rectitude is self evident. For something must be loved most of all, and it is none other than the highest good, even as this good is recognized by the intellect as that to which we must adhere the most."

[137]*Acceptatio* is the acceptance of a human act by God as a meritorious act. This will be detailed below.

[138]Ingham, *Scotus for Dunces*, at 230: "A general name for a per se being which has its ultimate actuality. In the case of a rational or intellectual nature, such a being is called a person. This term is a translation of hypostasis, the Greek term used to refer to the persons of the Trinity." See also her example at 110.

[139]See his *Lectura* discussion of *Ordinatio* I, 26

[140]Ingham, "John Duns Scotus: An Integrated Vision," 213. Ingham cites *Lectura* n.54.

[141]Ingham, "Integrated Vision," 214. Ingham cites *Quodlibet* 1.n.3 (Alluntis 1:5-6); trans. Alluntis/Wolter, 6-7.

[142]Ingham, "Integrated Vision," 217. Ingham cites *Quodlibet* 4.n.28 (Alluntis 4:61); trans. Alluntis/Wolter, 103-104.

[143]Ingham, "Integrated Vision," 218.

[144]Scotus, *Ordinatio* I.17.n.142 (Vatican 5:208); trans. Ingham, *Ethics and Freedom*, 217: "Here it can be said that in the meritorious act (about which we are now talking), I consider two, namely, that which precedes the notion of meritorious and in this level is included the substance of the act and its intensity and its moral

rectitude; beyond that, I consider the very notion itself of the meritorious which is to be accepted by the divine will relative to a reward or to be acceptable or worthy to be accepted." See also *Ordinatio* I. 17.n.144 (Vatican 5:208-09); trans. Ingham, *Ethics and Freedom*, 218: ". . . the aspect of merit is not completely had unless the aspect of worth is had or by being worthily able to be ordered to the reward (which is beatitude) and is worthily according to commutative or retributive justice . . . therefore, such order according to justice is only from the divine will gratuitously ordering, and so the aspect of merit will be completely from the divine will ordering this act toward the reward."

[145]Scotus, *Quodlibet 17*; trans. Alluntis/Wolter, 388-98.

[146]Fernand Guimet, "Conformité à la droît raison et possibilité surnaturelle de la charité," in *De Doctrina I. Duns Scoti*, vol. III, Acta Congressus Scotistici internationalis Oxonii et Edimburgi, ed. Camille Bérubé (Roma: Cura Commissionis Scotisticae, 1968), 539-97.

[147]Scotus, *Tractatus de primo principio*; trans. Wolter, *First Principle*, 2.

[148]Scotus, *Ordinatio* I.17.n.146 (Vatican 5:209); trans. Ingham, *Ethics and Freedom*, 223-24.

[149]Ingham, "Integrated Vision," 224. Ingham quotes her translation of *Ordinatio* I.d.17.n.146 (Vatican 5:209).

[150]Scotus, *Ordinatio* I.17.n.149 (Vatican 5, 210-11); trans. Ingham, *Ethics and Freedom*, 225.

[151]Ingham, "Integrated Vision," 226.

[152]See Louis Janssens, "Personalist Morals," *Louvain Studies* 8 (Spring 1980): 5-16. I find Janssens categories useful, though he uses Thomas Aquinas to support his assertions. In many instances, I think Franciscan theology more adequately supports the kinds of claims Janssens makes. However, the limits of this work do not allow me to elaborate this point.

[153]Boff, *Cry of the Earth, Cry of the Poor*, 53-6.

[154]Marcheschi, "Tabernacles," 5-7.

[155]See *The Pastoral Constitution on the Church in the Modern World*, especially Chapter 1. Various editions are available.

ABOUT THE AUTHOR

Dawn M. Nothwehr, O.S.F, a Franciscan Sister of Rochester, Minnesota, is Assistant Professor of Ethics at Catholic Theological Union in Chicago. She has a Master of Arts degree in Religious Studies from the Justice and Peace Institute of the Maryknoll School of Theology, where she specialized in feminist theology and theologies of liberation. She did her doctoral studies at Marquette University, where she was a Teaching Fellow (1993-94). She has taught theology at Quincy University, at St. Norbert College, De Pere, Wisconsin; at St. Xavier University, Chicago; and at St. Bernard's Institute, Colgate Divinity School, Rochester, New York. Her main interest is the ethics of power and the role of mutuality in the moral life. Her research is undergirded by significant experience in pastoral work with marginalized peoples, by diocesan social ministry and by the study and praxis of liberation theologies and feminist ethics. She is editor of *Franciscan Theology of the Environment: An Introductory Reader* (Quincy, IL: Franciscan Press, 2002) and author of *Mutuality: A Formal Norm for Christian Social Ethics* (San Francisco: Catholic Scholars Press, 1998), as well as numerous articles.